WILLIAM RANDOLPH
HEARST
Press Baron

WILLIAM RANDOLPH
HEARST
Press Baron

By

Nancy Frazier

THE AMERICAN DREAM

SILVER BURDETT PRESS
ENGLEWOOD CLIFFS, NEW JERSEY

Text © 1989 by Silver Burdett Press

Designed and produced by Blackbirch Graphics, Inc.

Project Editor: Nancy Furstinger

Manufactured in the United States of America

(Lib. ed.)   10   9   8   7   6   5   4   3   2   1

(Paper ed.)   10   9   8   7   6   5   4   3   2   1

Library of Congress Cataloging-in-Publication Data

Frazier, Nancy.
   William Randolph Hearst / by Nancy Frazier.
      (The American Dream)
   Bibliography: p. 124
   Includes index.
   Summary: A biography of well-known publisher of newspapers and magazines who developed a sensational journalistic style described by critics as "yellow journalism" and pioneered color comics, Sunday supplements, banner headlines, and editorial crusades.
      1. Hearst, William Randolph, 1863–1951—Juvenile literature. 2. Publishers and publishing—United States—Biography—Juvenile literature. 3. Newspaper publishing—United States—History—Juvenile literature. [1. Hearst, William Randolph, 1863–1951. 2. Publishers and publishing.]
   I. Title. II. Series: American Dream (Englewood Cliffs, N.J.)
   Z473.H38F73   1988   070'.92'4—dc19   [B]
   [92]   88-37560
                                                                        CIP
   ISBN 0-382-09585-5 (lib. bdg.)   AC
   ISBN 0-382-09593-6 (pbk.)

Contents

Introduction

Hearst, the Movie

*T*he music in the back-
ground is gloomy and haunting. A sign appears on
the screen—"No Trespassing." Behind the sign is a
pattern, the grid of a chain-link fence that leads to an
elaborate wrought iron gate. The initial K has been
forged onto the gate. On a hill in the distance,
behind the fence, is a castle—a dark, strange, tur-
reted mansion, rising through the mist. A light is on
in one of the high windows of the castle and, as the
camera draws closer, the window grows larger.

The audience seems to have gone through the
lighted window, but suddenly it is snowing—a
heavy, thick snowstorm that falls onto the roof of a
small house. As the camera draws back, it is revealed
that this little house is inside a glass ball, one of those
globes that become winter scenes when turned
upside down. All at once a full-lipped mouth and a
mustache fill the entire screen. The lips utter one

Opposite: *Orson Wells in* Citizen Kane (1941), *the film based on
the life of William Randolph Hearst.*

word, "Rosebud." The snowglobe falls to the floor and breaks. The man who spoke has died. A nurse walks into the room and pulls the sheet over him.

These scenes comprise the beginning of one of the most important films in history—*Citizen Kane*—about one of America's most noteworthy men. His name, in this version of the story, is Charles Foster Kane. Yet, from the moment the film was released in the 1940s, everyone knew that it was about a real man whose name was William Randolph Hearst.

In the movie, scenes of wild activity showed newspapers around the world telling of the death of this legendary millionaire. A newsreel—a documentary film that reported the news in movie theaters in the days before television—described his wealth: his estate on a private mountain, with a private zoo, his castle, and, as the newsreel commentator said, "a collection of everything—so big it can never be catalogued or appraised." Among Charles Kane's possessions are counted thirty-seven newspapers and two news syndicates, paper mills, apartment buildings, forests, and grocery stores. Kane was called "the greatest newspaper tycoon of this or any century."

How was the Kane empire built? The dates, the accomplishments, the trappings of Kane's life could be recorded, but the unsolved question remained: what kind of man was he? Did his dying word hold the clue? The plot of this film is the search by one reporter for the meaning of Kane's last word, "Rosebud."

In a key segment of the film, the action flashed back to an actual snowy day. The child Charles Kane is happily sledding and throwing snowballs at the sign in front of his house. The sign reads Mrs. Kane's Boarding House.

The scene inside the house was solemn. Kane's mother, who had become a wealthy woman after a boarder left her part ownership in a gold mine, had decided to send her son away. The father is portrayed as a drunkard who is likely to beat the boy. In the living room is the man whom Mrs. Kane has chosen to manage her finances and become Charles' guardian, a Mr. Thatcher. Mr. Thatcher had come to take Charles away. In the next wrenching scene Charles, with his precious sled clasped in this arms, pushes Mr. Thatcher into the snow.

At the age of twenty-five, Charles Kane inherited what was, by then, the world's sixth largest private fortune. But he cared little for any of it, except one thing, a newspaper—the *New York Inquirer*. "I think it would be fun to run a newspaper," he informed Mr. Thatcher.

So began the career of a man who moved into the editor's office and launched a colorful but controversial career. Under Kane's stewardship, the circulation of the *Inquirer* outstripped that of any other newspaper in the world. He poured money into the newspaper and, when he seems likely to lose everything during the great Depression of the 1930s, he said, prophetically, "You know . . . if I hadn't been born rich I might have been a very great man."

What happened, instead, was tragic. He lost everything that really mattered, including his best friend and his wife. In the end, he was alone in his enormous castle.

And what of "Rosebud"? The last scene in the movie is back inside the castle. A reporter has gone to talk to the butler, who heard Charles Kane's dying word. All the things that Kane had collected over the years—the statues, the paintings, the enormous collection of objects—are being sorted, priced, and crated. Some items are being discarded.

The camera moves in closer and closer to the objects, especially those that are being pitched into a blazing fireplace. A strangely familiar object is thrown into the fire and, while flames begin to lick the wooden frame, it can be recognized as the young Charles Kane's sled, the sled he was happily riding the day Mr. Thatcher came to take him away. Just as the sled goes up in flames, the brand name painted onto it appears: Rosebud.

Drums roll as dark smoke rises into the sky above the sinister castle. Once again the scene is outside the gate, and on the screen the sign that reads "No Trespassing" reappears.

It was just a movie, perhaps, but ever since *Citizen Kane* was made, there has been a powerful association between the fictional Charles Foster Kane and the real William Randolph Hearst in the public mind. Over the years the phrase "Rosebud" has become a code word, conjuring up the movie and the idea of a man who could have been great but was not; a man who could never be happy. Not many people know where fact ends and fiction begins. Rather, almost everyone who knows anything at all about Hearst and his empire associates him with the life and world they saw in *Citizen Kane*.

How much of this dramatic, sad, and strange story is true? The life of William Randolph Hearst and that of Charles Kane are similar in certain respects, but they are also very different. How clearly can we see the real man whose life unfolded behind the symbolic "No Trespassing" sign?

George Hearst, Forty-niner

*I*n January 1848, gold was discovered along the Sacramento River on land owned by a Swiss immigrant, John August Sutter. The news started the California Gold Rush. All over the country, all over the world, farmers dropped their hoes, sailors jumped ship, shopkeepers closed shop, and adventurers of every variety stopped what they were doing and headed for California. Blinded by visions of gold dust and dreams of great wealth, armies of fortune seekers made their way toward the Pacific during the next year. These seekers of wealth came to be called forty-niners.

In the year before the Gold Rush began, the population of California was 15,000. By 1852 it was 250,000. One of the newcomers was a man named George Hearst.

George Hearst was born in 1820 on a small plantation in the frontier country of Franklin, Missouri.

George Hearst, Forty-niner

George Hearst, William Randolph Hearst's father, went to California during the Gold Rush, and made his fortune in the Comstock Lode.

George was just twenty-six when his father died, and he worked hard to pay off the family debts and take care of his sister, brother, and mother.

Mining always fascinated George Hearst. Even as a boy he liked to spend time at the lead mine near his home, where he also worked part time. Though he had just two years of schooling and could barely read, he acquired a few geology books and studied them avidly. He talked with local miners, and watched and learned. The Indians who lived in that part of Missouri were impressed by George's knowledge of geology, and nicknamed him Boy-That-Earth-Talked-To.

On May 12, 1850, George Hearst and fifteen other fortune seekers headed for California. It was a hard journey from the sparsely settled eastern part of Missouri where they lived. Once they arrived in Independence, Missouri, in the northwest corner of the state, they probably joined a wagon train on the 2,000-mile-long Oregon Trail. The trail stretched from Independence to Astoria, Oregon, at the mouth of the Columbia River on the Pacific Ocean.

At Fort Laramie, Wyoming, the first permanent settlement in the state, Hearst became so sick with cramps, fever, diarrhea, and nausea that he wished himself dead. He was suffering from cholera, which was often fatal in those days. A weaker person would certainly have died.

George Hearst recovered and continued his journey west. He reached Eldorado County, California, by the end of the year, after about six months on the trail. In Spanish, El Dorado means "the gilded place," and is also the name of the imaginary kingdom sought by sixteenth-century Spanish explorers. At last, with pick and shovel, George began to dig. He endured great hardships, slept on the ground, and hunted for his food. If some inner voice had sent him westward, it was not to strike gold. For nine whole years he tried and failed. At one point he was so much in debt that, when he attempted to leave town on his mule, the local police officer took his transportation out from under him.

This was an era when far more hopes were dashed than were ever realized, a time when new towns were named Rough-n-Ready, Rattlesnake Bar, and Yankee Jim's. Still, more than a few fortunes were quickly made, not only in gold, but in all the businesses started to support and service the great westward migration. Henry Wells and William G. Fargo, for instance, realized that stagecoach and banking ventures would be profitable. The company they founded became as famous for its Wild West adventure stories as for its great wealth. Wells Fargo & Co., founded in 1852, survives today as a major, international banking institution, as well as an armored truck company.

No such good fortune shone on George Hearst. Not, at least, for nearly a decade. Luckily he was

Gold prospectors washing ore in a sluice box.

rescued by two friends, Melville Atwood and A.E. Head, who got his mule back for him. Then the three partners rode on to Virginia City, Nevada. They scraped together $450 to buy half a share in a mining claim called the Comstock Lode. (In mining, a lode is a fissure or crack in the rock that is filled with precious metal). The Comstock mine would become almost as legendary as Sutter's Mill. Comstock was a strike so rich that it started a silver rush nearly as feverish as the gold rush of 1849. Suddenly, George Hearst was a wealthy man. He bought into another mine and hit pay dirt once again.

In 1860, Hearst received the news that his mother was ill. George made his way home to Missouri. Hearst was forty years old by then, and by reputation, he had an uncanny sixth sense about mines—some miners and prospectors called him the best judge of a mine in the country. Many people said he could predict the value of a strike after no more than a quick trip undergound. In a cliché that had special meaning, it also was said that his word was as good as gold.

Back home tending to his mother, George was reintroduced to Phoebe Apperson, a pretty, delicate girl of eighteen. When George had last seen her, Phoebe had been just about old enough for piggyback rides. Now she was a teacher. She was refined. He was, frankly, crude. But if he was crude, at least he was handsome and rich. At first her parents said no when he asked to marry her, but finally the match was made. In June 1862, a year after the Civil War began, Phoebe Apperson married George Hearst in Stedman, Missouri. In October the couple left for California by a complicated but interesting route: they went by train to New York, then by ship to Panama, where they crossed the isthmus and boarded another ship for San Francisco. On April 29, 1863, Phoebe Hearst gave birth to a boy, who was named after his paternal and maternal grandfathers. His name was William Randolph Hearst.

Chapter 2

Early Influences

*In eighteen hundred and
  sixty-three
Life on this planet began
  for me
In the midst of the war of
  the North and South
The first sound issued
  from my small mouth.
On the wire, on the air,
  and in public prints
I've been arguing ever
  since.*

William Randolph Hearst was an adult when he dashed this verse off on a scratch pad. The lines let us know that he was aware, if not proud, of his tendency to jump right into the middle of a controversy—even to get a good fight going. What it doesn't say is why he was the way he was. This man, as powerful and wealthy as anyone could hope to be, was also an enigma. He remains so to all who try to explain his behavior.

The movie *Citizen Kane* suggests that sending the young boy away from home, depriving him of his parents' love, launched him on his lonely pursuit of love and power. Such was not the case with William Randolph Hearst.

William was, indeed, born with a silver spoon in his mouth. But he was not sent away from a stern but protective mother and unreliable father, as was his movie counterpart. On the contrary, Hearst's mother doted on him and kept him constantly by her side. "Bless his little heart," she wrote in letters to relatives and friends about Willie, as she called him. "He is a very good boy . . . . He seems to understand everything . . . . His being with me so constantly has made him perfectly devoted to me. He never wants anyone else to do anything for him, and I think I love him better than ever before. Some days I do very little but amuse him. He is very wise and sweet . . . he is a great comfort to me."

If young Hearst wasn't cut off from his parents' love, are there any clues to his later behavior? Is, in fact, his mother's smothering devotion and attention a clue? One of Hearst's biographers, W.A. Swanberg, has written: "He was mothered, loved, pampered, praised, protected, instructed, fussed over, waited on, and worried about every minute of his infant existence." Swanberg suggests that the boy received far too much attention and was spoiled by that.

His father, George Hearst, was not so excessively attentive. He was often out of town and was certainly preoccupied with his mining interests, his expanding business ventures—he went into ranching, raising cattle, and breeding horses—and his political career. George Hearst's properties were spread from Montana to Mexico. And he became a senator, first in California and then in the Congress of the United States.

Senator George Hearst was tall and wiry and had a grisly beard. He was a salty fellow, nicknamed "Uncle George," jovial and good-hearted. He was a gambler and a storyteller. Stories were told about him, too.

One tale about "Uncle George" describes how he'd stop at his company's cashier on the way to lunch and ask for "a bag of clinkers." On the street he'd pass by a group of down-and-out prospectors who were called, ironically, the Sunshine Club. George Hearst would greet each man by name and shake every hand that was thrust out. As he did so,

*Phoebe Apperson Hearst,
William Randolph
Hearst's mother, was his
constant companion
during his childhood.*

he'd slip one of those "clinkers," a gold piece, into the fellow's palm.

Senator Hearst was as well known for his sense of humor as for his generosity. Californians repeated his comment, "Why gamble unless you bet mor'n you can afford," and loved tales about his one-upmanship. As one story goes, George met in the daytime with a group of other wealthy men in a private room on the ground floor of the old Palace Hotel in San Francisco. There they would play friendly games of poker in which the stakes were not high. One day a boastful Easterner saw them through the open door and walked in. To show off his wealth, he threw a $100 bill on the table, assuming he'd make a grand impression. George Hearst, who was "banker" for that round, handed the fellow a single white chip for his money, pretending that a $100 bill was the smallest denomination they played with. Nothing else could have put that Easterner in his place quite so effectively.

George Hearst drank bourbon, chewed tobacco, and played up his own raw edges: "My opponents say I haven't the book-learning that they possess," he told a gathering at the California Democratic convention in 1882. "They say I can't spell. They say I spell bird, b-u-r-d. If b-u-r-d doesn't spell bird, what in the hell does it spell?"

Phoebe Apperson Hearst was as delicate as George her husband was rough, as refined as he was coarse. She had taught school before her marriage and firmly believed in the value of education. When Willie was ten she took him and a tutor, a young Harvard graduate named Thomas Barry, to Europe.

Their trip began in the spring of 1873 with a journey on the transcontinental railroad that had been completed just four years earlier. In those days, travelers on the railroad kept a sharp eye out for Indians and took shots at buffalo and deer from the train windows. When they got to Boston, Phoebe, Willie, and Thomas boarded a ship called the *Adriatic* for their voyage across the Atlantic.

Willie and his mother met up with friends in Europe and spent an entire year traveling. They visited museums, toured castles, learned German and French, and bought many treasures, ranging from postage stamps to statues. Willie was acquiring tastes that lasted him all of his life.

In Rome, Phoebe Hearst arranged an audience with Pope Pius IX. "He was so kind and lovely, spoke altogether in French, asked where we came from," she wrote home to her husband. "When he came to Willie he placed his hand on his head and blessed him . . ."

As for Willie, he enjoyed the culture, the collecting, the education, and he also enjoyed the havoc he created. For, by this time in his life, young William Randolph Hearst had already shown a very strong tendency to cause mischief.

Chapter 3

A Fondness for Fireworks

When Phoebe Hearst wrote friends and relatives about domestic matters, or about her travels with Willie, she usually didn't describe her son's bouts of troublemaking. She alluded to that once, though, in a letter to her husband, when her son was sick. She wrote: "He talked so quietly and was very good; but I would have felt happier to have him well and a *little* bad."

How bad was Willie? If his mother avoided discussing his youthful adventures, they were talked about by others. Even the grown-up William Randolph Hearst, in moments of nostalgia, liked to write about them. When he was in his seventies, he started writing a column for his newspapers called "In the News." In this column, Hearst called himself "Little Willie" and often came up with a humorous moral at the end of the story about his exploit. The following are some excerpts from "In the News."

Out of the far past come memories to your columnist of Little Willie . . . .

When Willie was a small boy he was always getting into trouble, most of which he made for himself, but not exclusively for himself . . . .

Once . . . Willie's mama and papa were having their house "done over" and were debating—in view of Willie's troublemaking qualities—what they were going to do with Willie . . . .

They had all been invited to stay at the home of the Addisons . . . (who had a delightful place on Nob Hill and were exceedingly nice, quiet people. . . .)

On the whole Willie was painfully and portentously well-behaved until the First of April came along.

Then Willie felt that something ought to be done to relieve the monotony of this serene household and to prevent himself from degenerating into a sissy.

So when everyone was out of the Addison house or duly occupied within it, Willie shook what money he had out of his bank, sauntered forth, and bought a half a dozen Bengal lights at a fireworks shop.

Bengal lights, as everyone knows, flare up in red fire and have, at a little distance, every semblance of a considerable conflagration.

Willie then borrowed a half a dozen tin pie plates from the Addisons' cook and hid the lights and pie plates under the bed in his pleasant and peaceful room. . . .

Willie waited until he was sufficiently sure that everybody was asleep and then dragged the pie plates and the Bengal lights out from under the bed— arranged the Bengal lights on the pie plates and set off the fireworks.

Then he opened the door and shrieked down the silent halls of the sleeping house: "Fire! Fire! Fire!"

Willie locked himself in his room.

The firetrucks were called and just about when one of the firemen on a ladder was prying open the window to rescue him, Willie unlocked his door, went into the hall, and gleefully announced that he was just playing an April Fool's joke.

His indulgent mother was so grateful he was alive and well that she barely said anything. His father was less forgiving.

"Were you very warm in that room while the fire was going on, Willie?"

"No, Papa, I wasn't warm at all," said Willie.

"Well," said Papa, laying Willie across his knee, bottomside up, "you're going to be warmed now, son, where it will do you the most good."

The adult columnist, looking back on his youth, adds this comment:

> But with all his pretense of severity, Willie's papa never did warm Willie as he deserved.
>
> If he had done so Willie might have grown up to be a better—columnist.

In another of his columns, Hearst described his childhood fantasy of being a pirate, and the outrage he felt at being sent to dancing school—enough outrage to provoke him to throw a large stone through the window of the school.

"Willie never realized his ambition to be a pirate, but he got to be a newspaperman, which is in the same general category," was Hearst's tongue-in-cheek conclusion to the story.

As for his European pranks, they were also explosive. In one instance he and his friend, Eugene Lent—Genie—used a little brass cannon to shoot at pigeons, but the powder ignited and burned Willie's hand. Mrs. Hearst was told that if she soaked his hand in alcohol it would get better.

"That *was* a mistake," Hearst later wrote.

> The burned hand soon stopped aching and Willie looked around the room for pleasurable occupation.
>
> On the mantlepiece was a fine small model of a ship under a glass globe.
>
> "Say, Genie," said Willie, "let's have a fire at sea." So Genie took the ship from under the globe and floated it in the basin of alcohol, and Willie got some matches and lighted the alcohol.
>
> The fire at sea was a spectacular success until the bowl cracked and the flaming alcohol flowed all over the floor.
>
> Then the fire on land began to attract universal attention.
>
> Genie, in calling for help, managed to dislodge one of the green shutters of the back window, which fell

William Randolph Hearst was eight years old when this formal portrait was made in 1871.

through the glass roof of the kitchen beneath and put Mme. Pincée's chef in the hospital.

The scene was made complete by the arrival of the brass-helmeted *pompiers* of the Paris fire department, who drowned out the fire and also drowned out most of Mme. Pincée's guests on the floor below.

If the Willie stories begin to have a theme, it is the refrain of a boy doing everything he can to draw attention to himself. Throughout his life, fireworks had a special attraction. Not many things make as much of a show and so much noise. There had been fireworks at the farewell parties that were thrown before Willie and his mother left for Europe; and there were fireworks at many other events and celebrations he staged as he grew older.

There was another side to Willie, though, one that is often omitted in discussions about his youth. This side is the sensitive boy, whose feelings are more difficult to document. Mrs. Hearst alluded to this side of Willie in another letter to her husband, written while she and Willie were in Europe: "The poorer classes are so terribly poor. Willie wanted to give away all his money and clothes, too, and really I felt the same way, if we could have relieved even half of them."

Still, if the distressing sight of poverty, such as he had never witnessed in the United States, troubled him, it didn't take the edge off of his own extravagant tastes. He had money to buy most of what struck his fancy. Upon seeing Windsor Castle, in England, he was heard to say, "I would like to live there." Indeed, before he died William Randolph Hearst did own several castles.

If the child is father to the man, this child was full of mischief, loved to be the center of attention, and enjoyed works of art and intellectual stimulation. He was as boisterous as his father and as curious as his mother.

Chapter 4

School Shenanigans

*I*n 1879, Phoebe, Willie, and Thomas Barry took a second grand tour of Europe—another round of sightseeing and collecting. During this trip, Mrs. Hearst became ill and went to one of Germany's spas for a cure. She sent Willie back to the United States and had him enrolled in St. Paul's, a private school in Concord, New Hampshire. Before he went to St. Paul's, Willie had attended four different schools in San Francisco. Whether he left by choice or was expelled is anyone's guess. The records of all those schools were lost in the great San Francisco fire of 1906.

New England and prep school were culture shock for Willie, who was sixteen by now and a tall, gangly young man. Traveling and visiting places away from home with his mother was one thing, but having to live in unfamiliar surroundings and to abide by the rules and regulations of an institution was quite another.

Hearst and his mother were among the ten million visitors to the Centennial Exposition in Philadelphia in 1876.

Willie Hearst was unhappy at the school in Concord. He chafed under its strict discipline and he disliked and poked fun at the Anglophile traditions:

> The school had a carefully groomed English lawn, such as one might see at Harrow or Rugby or Eton (three esteemed, aristocratic British schools) or almost anywhere along the good old Thames, don't you know.
>
> And on the spick-and-span and much mowed lawn one was supposed to play cricket, and one did with a ball as hard as a cobble rock and a bat as flat as a Hollywood tenor's high C.
>
> One got to be fairly good at the jolly game, too, but one never really liked it because there was no adjacent window to knock the bally ball through and, consequently, no sufficiently positive method of tallying the score.

Those are the words of an older man looking back on his youth and complaining of an institution putting on airs. Whether those pretensions bothered him at the time he was there, or whether he was just lonesome and homesick, is difficult to say. Willie did write his mother, who was still recuperating in Germany, "If you get well, you shall never have anything to make you sick again, if I can help it . . . . I often think how bad I have been and how many unkind words I have said, and I am sure that when you come back I will . . . never be so bad again."

Promises, promises. In 1881, Willie was expelled from St. Paul's for reasons that have never been made public, but most likely were connected to some new brand of mischief or disobedience. Once back in San Francisco, Willie studied with private tutors and probably paid at least a visit or two to the office of the *San Francisco Examiner.* Willie's father had become owner of the San Francisco newspaper in 1880, after lending its publishers money that they were unable to repay. An interest in printing was developing in William Randolph Hearst.

Phoebe Hearst had specific educational goals for her son. On her way home from Germany, while

Willie was still enrolled at St. Paul's, she had stopped on the East Coast long enough to take him to visit Harvard University. Or, as Hearst himself later wrote, "Willie's mama stopped in Boston, partly to see friends there, and partly to give Willie a glimpse of Harvard and show him where he might wind up if he did not mend his ways—and he did not mend his ways."

William Randolph Hearst was nineteen when he entered Harvard in 1882. His room was in Matthews Hall, a five-story, red brick building that had been finished just ten years before Hearst arrived. It was also the first building on the campus to have bathtubs, all of which were in the basement.

When Willie moved in, his mother hired a decorator, added a library, and had lavish furnishings provided for her boy Willie. Even the well-to-do sons of Harvard were dazzled and dazed by the excess. But, once again Willie was homesick: "I am beginning to get awfully tired of this place," he wrote his mother, "and I long to get out West somewhere where I can stretch myself without coming in contact with the narrow walls with which the prejudice of the bean eaters has surrounded us. I long to get out in the woods and breathe the fresh mountain air and listen to the moaning of the pines. It makes me almost crazy with homesickness when I think of it. I hate this weak, pretty New England scenery with its gentle rolling hills, its pea green foliage, its vistas. . . . I long to see our own woods, the jagged rocks and towering mountains, the majestic pines, the grand impressive scenery of the far West. I shall never live anywhere but in California. I like to be away for a while only to appreciate it the more when I return."

He was suffering the pangs of separation, but he also put too much of his energy into cutting up and attracting attention. He kept an alligator named Champagne Charlie on a leash, played banjo, and joined all the clubs. In 1884, to celebrate the election of Grover Cleveland as 22nd president of the United States, Willie staged an all-night party, which was lit up with his favorite party treat—fireworks. He hired a brass band and bought wagonloads of beer. He hung a huge banner, with portraits of Cleveland and the vice president-elect, from the boardinghouse where he lived, and topped the exceedingly loud affair with roosters that crowed through the early hours of the morning.

Cleveland had run for office on a platform of reform and had made it clear that the interests of rich and powerful industrialists were not necessarily his own. He was especially displeased when those interests were promoted at the expense of the great masses of working people. For example, Cleveland opposed the "protective tariff," or tax, on merchandise imported from foreign countries. The protective tariff pleased American manufacturers because it gave them an advantage over foreign suppliers in that they could sell their merchandise more cheaply than imported goods. They could also increase their own profits after removing the foreign competition. Protective tariffs did not, however, favor the pocketbooks of ordinary American consumers who had to pay the higher prices. To Cleveland and to young Hearst, who agreed with Cleveland, these tariffs were unfair.

Hearst's enthusiastic support of Cleveland, the first political consciousness he showed in any major way, revealed the direction his own sympathies were taking at the time. However, the manner in which he displayed his support—that night of wild celebration—got him suspended from Harvard for a few months. During this temporary leave of Cambridge, Willie Hearst visited Washington, D.C., where he attended sessions of Congress, studied American history, and went to the inauguration of his hero, President Cleveland. It was his first brush with the most powerful position in the country.

Chapter 5

Ink in His Veins

*B*y the age of twenty-one, William Randolph Hearst was 6 feet 2 inches tall, and had blond hair and light blue eyes, which were sometimes described as icy blue. He had a flair for dressing with flamboyance. His clothes were fashionable, but he always added a bold touch, often with brightly colored cravats or boldly patterned waistcoats.

The way he dressed, the things he did, and the ideas he had were flashy. Considering his attention-getting exploits and outfits, it might be expected that he was loud and unruly. He was, instead, extraordinarily shy; his voice was high-pitched and soft, more like that of a woman or young boy than a man.

When William Hearst was allowed to return to Harvard University in 1885, he continued his extravagances and his ridiculous pranks. He was not a very good student—in his first year he had dropped both

Greek and Latin, and tried philosophy, which he also dropped. But, during his second year he developed an interest in the *Harvard Lampoon,* the nation's oldest college humor magazine. This interest provided useful direction for some of his energy.

The *Lampoon* had been started in Room M 17 of Matthews Hall, in 1876, and was still published in students' quarters when Hearst arrived at Harvard. The *Lampoon's* business manager was his good friend, Eugene Lent, the same Genie of Paris pranks, but the financial health of the magazine was poor. Hearst took on the challenge of rescuing the *Lampoon* and pulled off his first major business success. He went around town to the shops where he was already known as a big spender and talked the owners into advertising in the *Lampoon.* He organized a group of students to sell more advertising space. He wrote to Harvard grads and parents of Harvard men asking for their support. He mounted a circulation drive that was also a big success. Not only did he get the *Lampoon* out of the red, he got it into the black—it became profitable for the first time in its history.

Hearst added some of his typical bon vivant showmanship to this job. He rented a room on Brattle Street for the magazine, equipped it with a long table, chairs, and a stove and gave keys to *Lampoon* staff members. He also subscribed to the leading newspapers in the country, which led to his becoming intrigued with a paper published in New York City called the *New York World.* "Say fellows," he once asked his cohorts, "do you know who's running the best paper in the country? It's a man named Pulitzer down in New York. I have been studying his methods and I think I have caught on to what he's trying to do. Maybe I'll start a paper and give you fellows a job."

Most members of the *Lampoon* staff enjoyed the luxury of their new quarters and the boisterous extravagance of their business manager. One holdout was George Santayana, who later became a famous philosopher and poet. He turned the key to the *Lampoon* office down in disgust. Santayana had joined the magazine as a cartoonist, but he was not amused by Hearst's activities.

Ink was beginning to run thickly through William Hearst's veins. While on suspension, he had written his father a long letter about the *San Francisco Examiner*, the paper George Hearst owned, and how it should be run. "I have begun to have a strange fondness for our little paper—a tenderness like unto that which a mother feels for a puny or deformed offspring, and I should hate to see it die now after it had battled so long and so nobly for existence; in fact, to tell the truth, I am possessed of the weakness which at some time or other of their lives pervades most men; I am convinced that I could run a newspaper successfully."

William went on to tell his father some of the steps he would take to improve the appearance, the writing, the circulation, and the reputation of the *Examiner*. His own style peeks through his recommendations when he writes: "And now to close with a suggestion of great consequence; namely, that all these changes be made not by degrees but all at once so that the improvement will be very marked and noticeable and will attract universal attention and comment."

Once again, William Hearst was after the grand, startling, attention-grabbing gesture. No chance of progress by slow, careful steps for him, no removing obstacles with care—he went in for dynamite. This young man, although usually described as quiet and painfully shy, believed in explosives to move molehills and mountains alike.

In addition to his interest in the *Harvard Lampoon*, William Hearst's attention had been drawn to the *Boston Globe*. Much as his father once hung around the lead mines in his hometown of Franklin County, Missouri, learning what he could on the

✳

"I am possessed of the weakness which at some time or other of their lives pervades most men; I am convinced I could run a newspaper successfully."

spot by watching, asking questions, and teaching himself the ways and means of mining, so young William Randolph Hearst began to teach himself the workings of the one thing he loved with unsurpassed passion—newspaper publishing. He began to educate himself about every facet of that profession.

The Harvard days came to a premature end due, once again, to one of Willie's pranks. He had chamber pots, each with the name of one of his teachers painted on the bottom inside, delivered to the teachers' homes. That was the last straw. Hearst was expelled from Harvard. Not only was he expelled, but he was *expunged*. His name is to be found nowhere in the University's official records. For Harvard, William Randolph Hearst never existed. It was the most serious step the institution could take against any student.

When he left Harvard, Hearst took with him the invaluable experience he'd gained during his business stewardship of the *Harvard Lampoon*. He had had his first publishing coup. He'd shown how effectively his energy and imagination could bring success when he put his mind to something. And he was determined to devote his professional life to the newspapers, although that was not at all what his father had in mind for his only child. William Randolph Hearst was obsessed with becoming a newspaperman.

Once Hearst left Harvard, he left many of his youthful excesses behind: he didn't smoke or drink or create much mischief, at least not on a local scale. He had more important things to do. He went to New York City to start his career and got a job as a reporter at the *World*, the paper that had captured his fascination. Neither his mother, who would have liked him to become a diplomat, nor his father, who wanted the young man to take charge of one of the other family business interests, was pleased by William's decision. But he persisted and continued writing his father letters filled with advice about what to do with the *Examiner.*

This era, the 1880s, was one of tremendous change and social upheaval. The railroads were being built to crisscross the country, and telegraph lines ran alongside them. After 13 years under construction, the greatest suspension bridge in the world, the Brooklyn Bridge, was opened. The Industrial Revolution was in full swing.

While a few men became rich and powerful, the multitudes who worked for them were often unfairly exploited. To protect these workers, labor unions grew in membership and power. In 1886, the year that William Hearst started work at the New York *World*, the Statue of Liberty, a gift from France to America, was raised in New York Harbor. In that same year, 1886, labor riots and strikes broke out all across the country.

Joseph Pulitzer, owner of the New York *World*, became a major inspirational force in the life of William Randolph Hearst. Pulitzer's life story itself is a rags-to-riches success story. Pulitzer was seventeen and penniless when he arrived in the United States in 1864. He served as a private in the First New York Cavalry during the Civil War. He then moved to St. Louis and began his career in both journalism and politics. At first a liberal Republican, Pulitzer changed party affiliation after his group was unable to win the presidency for their candidate, Horace Greeley. As a Democrat, Pulitzer ran unsuccessfully for Congress. As a publisher, his first great success was the *St. Louis Post-Dispatch*, which became one of the most prominent, influential, and profitable newspapers in the West.

Pulitzer took over the New York *World* in 1882, just four years before William Hearst went to work there. In the first edition of the newspaper published under his charge, Pulitzer proclaimed, "There is room in this great and growing city for a journal that is not only cheap but bright, not only bright but

Joseph Pulitzer (1847–1911), the newspaper editor and publisher, was Hearst's hero, and later his rival.

large, not only large but truly democratic—dedicated to the cause of the people rather than to that of the purse potentates—devoted more to the news of the New World than the Old World—that will expose all fraud and sham, fight all public evils and abuses—that will battle for the people with earnest sincerity."

In 1885, Pulitzer was elected to Congress from New York. However, failing health and impending blindness forced him to resign his seat. Before he died in 1911, Pulitzer had endowed the School of Journalism at Columbia University and established the Pulitzer Prizes, the most coveted and controversial prizes in journalism.

When Pulitzer took over the *World*, its circulation was 20,000. By the time Hearst went to work for him in 1886, the circulation had climbed to 250,000. Hearst was there when Pulitzer had a silver medal struck to commemorate "the largest circulation ever attained by an American newspaper." It is no wonder young William was impressed. He studied the methods Pulitzer used: crusading journalism, promotional stunts (like raising the money needed to erect the Statue of Liberty), and eye-catching design elements, including woodcut illustrations. Pulitzer adapted new ideas for graphic illustration. For example, a story about a murder might include maps and diagrams drawn to show where the murder took place and where the body was found.

If Pulitzer could achieve success with such stunts why, William Randolph Hearst must have wondered, couldn't he?

Chapter 6

Crowning the Monarch

George Hearst didn't want his son to be a newspaperman. He planned to sell the *Examiner* to a political enemy, because the paper was so unprofitable. He offered William the opportunity to develop any of the ranches or mines in his possession, but William Randolph Hearst was determined. He wanted to run the *Examiner*.

George Hearst had been appointed to complete a term in the United States Senate for a senator from California who had died. In 1887, he was elected to that post in his own right and was facing a six-year term in Washington, D.C. It was at this time that he decided to give in to his son and offer him the *Examiner*.

Though many San Franciscans said the best thing you could use the *Examiner* for was to light a fire, William Hearst, not yet twenty-four years old, was overjoyed to own it. It was exactly what he wanted. When he took charge on March 4, 1887, the circulation was approximately 24,000. Many of those copies were not even sold but were given away— George Hearst's primary interest in the paper had been to use it for promoting his own political ambitions.

Immediately, William Randolph Hearst turned the *Examiner* into a news carnival, a theatrical production in which the human sideshow was ever changing, ever more bizarre, tragic, sinful, humorous, or glamorous. In the very first issue published under his authority, the front page story about abandoned children was guaranteed to bring a tear to the eye. Another story in that same issue contained a lot of unpleasant details from the testimony in a divorce case; unpleasant, perhaps, but guaranteed to draw attention to the newspaper.

Before long the *Examiner* had a column called "The Workingman," in which activities of the labor unions were reported. At the same time, crusades against devious officials, public and private, were begun. A new city charter, with the express purpose of strengthening the control of the political bosses, came under attack by the *Examiner* and, to Hearst's credit, was defeated.

Collis Potter Huntington (1821–1900) was one of the founders of the Central Pacific and Southern Pacific railroads.

The Southern Pacific railroad company, run by Collis P. Huntington and his partner Leland Stanford, received special attention in the Hearst crusade. *Examiner* forces were mobilized against the Southern Pacific. As rich and powerful as Hearst became, however, he was always a lightweight next to the monopolistic, monolithic power of the railroad. The Southern Pacific routinely used bribery as a tool to buy favorable government regulations, while at the same time it charged exorbitant rates to shippers. Moreover, the railroad provided poor service for its customers.

Any complaints against the railroad or disasters it experienced, from late trains to crashes, were played up in the *Examiner.* Ambrose Bierce, a sharp-tongued writer who was greatly admired by Hearst, joined the *Examiner* staff and was particularly alert to what the Southern Pacific officials did. He would always substitute a dollar sign for the initial S in Leland Stanford's last name.

Stanford and Huntington borrowed millions and millions of dollars from the government to build the railroad, and they were continuously looking for ways to avoid paying their debts. They declared that the Southern Pacific would go bankrupt if they had to honor their financial obligations. In one of his columns, Bierce scolded Stanford for buying his wife a $100,000 necklace, spending millions on race-horses, works of art, and land, as well as giving $30 million to found a university at a time he owed the government—in reality the American people—so much money. Today, Stanford University is one of the nation's top schools of higher education.

Hearst became irate if another newspaper got a story before his paper had it. In one adventure an *Examiner* reporter not only scooped the other papers, but he made both the police and the Southern Pacific officials look foolish. The scoop occurred at the time a series of train robberies were being committed by a couple of bandits. These two men had the sympathy of many ordinary people, because public opinion held the railroad moguls in low regard. An *Examiner* reporter went off by himself into the woods where the bandits were hiding. He interviewed them and published the story, embarrassing the railroad, the police, and the other San Francisco papers.

This sort of journalism was sensationalism at its liveliest. And Hearst's political stand was made crystal clear: he was for union labor, the eight-hour day, and income tax. He was against cheap labor brought in from China—often to work on the railroads. The San Franciscans on Nob Hill, often called Snob Hill, began to look askance at Hearst.

Hearst's reporters didn't sit around waiting for news to happen. They went to great lengths to get,

Leland Stanford (1824–1893), a former governor of California, was a major shareholder in many railroad construction companies and president of the Southern Pacific Company.

and even to create, their stories. In order to write about what it was like to be institutionalized, one reporter jumped off a steamboat and behaved irrationally when he was rescued. He was committed to a mental institution and then wrote about it from an insider's point of view.

A reporter whose real name was Winifred Sweet wrote under the byline of Annie Laurie. "Annie" became known as the first "sob sister," because her ability to write so movingly brought tears to readers' eyes. Once dressed like a homeless person, "Annie" pretended to faint on the street. Her exposé of the cruel treatment that people, especially women, received in the emergency room of a hospital made readers' flesh crawl. Besides shocking the public, Annie Laurie's exposés resulted in changes in policy and personnel at the hospital to which she was taken. Her writing also brought about a much needed service, the establishment of regular ambulance service.

For another article, Annie Laurie got a job and reported on working conditions in a fruit cannery. Once she told the story of a crippled child so dramatically that a charitable fund was started and thousands of dollars were raised toward a hospital.

Many of Hearst's friends and former co-workers on the *Harvard Lampoon* were hired to work for the *Examiner.* One of these people, a writer named E.D. "Phinney" Thayer wrote the famous baseball poem, "Casey at the Bat" for the *Examiner.*

Hearst added a tag line to his newspaper's name: he called it the "Monarch of the Dailies." And if William Randolph Hearst was the king of the Monarch, at least it wasn't his style to sit back on his throne and give orders. He worked with his employees in every department of the paper, from setting type to writing headlines.

Another significant characteristic of Hearst as an employer was that he didn't stint on salaries. On the contrary, when he hired someone he admired, he paid that person a handsome salary by anyone's standard. And such policies got results: after his very first year as owner, the paper had twice as many advertisers as before he took over, and its circulation had nearly doubled.

"His knowledge and activities were not confined solely to the editorial and news departments of a newspaper. He was equally thoroughly conversant with the functioning of all departments of his news-

Market Street in San Francisco at the turn of the century. A frontier town with a population of 200 in 1846, San Francisco had a third of a million people by 1900.

paper properties," wrote Edmond D. Coblentz, who worked for Hearst for more than 50 years. "A complete volume could be compiled of Mr. Hearst's instructions over the years to his editors, publishers, mechanical superintendents, advertising directors, and circulation managers."

Hearst's personal style was soft-spoken and polite. He always said "please" and "if you don't mind" when he asked someone to do something. He was full of praise and appreciation for good work, and he never fired anyone, no matter how clearly they deserved to be dismissed.

When a reporter named Alfonso "Blinker" Murphy was fired by the city editor, Murphy refused to go. "Mr. Murphy, it has always been my understanding that it was the right of the editor to discharge a man if he felt it necessary. Do you have any reason for suggesting that we make an exception?" Hearst asked when the incident was brought to his attention.

"I have, Mr. Hearst," Blinker Murphy answered. *"I refuse to be fired."*

Instead of losing his temper or exercising his authority, Hearst took this defiance with good humor and said to the city editor, "In the circumstances . . . I don't see what we can do about this." The editor also saw the amusing side of the situation, and Blinker Murphy worked at the *Examiner* for years after that.

For Hearst, journalism was an adventure, and every day brought something new and exciting. He encouraged a spirit of camaraderie in the newsroom. Sometimes he'd gather the staff to go out and fly kites, set off firecrackers and balloons, or go fishing, horseback riding, or sailing with him. With his enthusiasm, charm, generosity, sense of adventure, and tolerance for eccentricity, William Randolph Hearst was an unusual and well-liked employer. He was, however, equally feared and disliked by many outside the *Examiner* offices.

Chapter 7

Greener Pastures and Yellow Journalism

*B*y the time he celebrated his first year with the *San Francisco Examiner* in March 1888, William Randolph Hearst could boast that he had doubled the newspaper's circulation. Besides hiring the best writers he could find, he had also spent huge amounts of money modernizing the entire operation.

Prior to 1800, news-gathering was haphazard. News sources generally consisted of gossip and clippings from other papers, some of which were from other British colonies. Most of the important events, even those of historical significance, went unreported or misreported. In the early 1800s, the importance of getting news, and getting it first, led to excesses. For instance, instead of waiting for ships to unload, the New York papers sent reporters out in rowboats to meet them. Later, the *New York Herald* and *New York Morning Journal* went so far as to buy

A cylinder newspaper press was one of the technological advances put forward by Hearst.

schooners to meet incoming ships far out in the Atlantic. The expensive competition for getting news from Europe led, eventually, to pooling resources and starting the first cooperative news service. That news service became the Associated Press (AP), a news syndicate. Foreign news was delivered from port cities by fast riders on horseback. After the Atlantic cable was established, the telegraph became an invaluable instrument in the transmission of news.

For the first 150 years of newspaper publishing in America, all operations were carried out by hand. Presses were hand-operated. Type—the written information—was set by hand, letter by letter. For some time, even the paper was made by hand.

During the latter half of the nineteenth century, and into the twentieth century, technological advances were made in all phases of the newspaper industry, from printing and typesetting to paper and ink manufacture. As this technology became available, Hearst acquired the very latest, up-to-date machinery and equipment for the *Examiner.*

By October 1889, two years after Hearst took charge, the daily circulation of the *Examiner* was 55,000, an increase of more than 20,000. The number of pages in each issue of the paper was increasing, and it was about to show a profit for the first time. A little more than a year after that momentous event, on February 29, 1891, the front page of the *Examiner* was bordered in black ink to call attention to the death of Senator George Hearst.

George Hearst's obituary gave an account of his life, describing how he had started in mining with a pick and shovel on his shoulder. He left a fortune of $17 million, which he willed to his wife. His son and only child, William Randolph, was terribly unhappy to learn that he would not immediately inherit the money he needed to move his publishing ambitions forward. Instead, he would have to depend upon his mother, Phoebe, to help him finance his plans.

Before embarking on his new business ventures, Hearst took some time off to travel to Europe and Egypt on a long sightseeing and collecting trip. During this trip, he and his traveling companion, a man who worked for the paper, took thousands of photographs, and Hearst bought Egyptian mummies in addition to the more standard kinds of treasures he usually sought. Upon his return he persuaded his mother to help him finance the purchase of the *New York Morning Journal*. She sold her interest in the Anaconda Mine and turned over $7.5 million to him.

On September 25, 1895, William Randolph Hearst, age 32, became owner of the *New York Morning Journal*. Now Hearst was playing in the big leagues, against the man who had been his model and inspiration—Joseph Pulitzer. Hearst brought some of his top people to New York from California, and then he began raiding the staff of all the other newspapers, especially Pulitzer's *World*. He used his 11th-floor, California redwood-paneled office in the building Pulitzer owned to hire people from the *World's* editorial staff, offering to double salaries.

When Hearst took over the *Journal*, its circulation was 77,000. The *World's* circulation was 500,000. It did look like David next to Goliath—but not for

"The Yellow Kid" became a familiar figure in newspapers and was used by political cartoonists who were against Hearst's and Pulitzer's policies.

long. Hearst lowered the price of the *Journal* to one cent and increased its size to 16 pages. In the areas reporting crime and by using startling graphic art, bigger and bolder headlines, bigger pictures and livelier, saucier stories, Hearst out-Pulitzered Pulitzer.

The newpaper war was on, and the young upstart was gaining ground on the old general. In that first year, Hearst celebrated a major victory when he forced Pulitzer to lower the price of the *World* to one cent in order to stay competitive with the *Journal*.

Another major coup was the hiring of the *World's* Sunday editor, Morrill Goddard, who was known for cooking up incredible, circulation-building schemes.

"Your proposition might interest me, Mr. Hearst," Goddard had said when Hearst first offered him a job, "but I don't want to change a certainty for an uncertainty. Frankly I doubt if you will last three months in this town."

A draft on Wells Fargo & Co. for $35,000 made out to Goddard convinced him that Hearst was serious. Goddard came to the *Journal* and brought his key staff members with him. At one point Pulitzer almost succeeded in rehiring them, but they stayed at the *Journal,* making it notorious for lurid, steamy, and fantastic stories illustrated by pen and ink sketches.

As a headhunter, Hearst had no peer. In his corporate raid on the *World* , he brought to the *Journal* a cartoonist named Richard F. Outcault. Outcault had created a character known as the Yellow Kid, a youngster with big ears and funny toes who wears a yellow dress. The Yellow Kid was so popular that when Outcault left, Pulitzer got another artist, George B. Luks, to draw another Yellow Kid for the *World*. From this battle of the cartoon characters is derived the phrase that came to symbolize the kind of sensational newspapers that Pulitzer and Hearst were publishing: yellow journalism.

Stoking the Fires of War

Who can separate an individual's passion for justice from his wish to have his way? His championship of the underdog from his desire to topple the powerful? Or his desire to reveal truth, as he sees it, and drive to mold minds and move people to action?

William Randolph Hearst is an enigma. There is no doubt that his heart and sympathies were with the underprivileged people whose plights were written about in his newspapers. He is criticized for the means he used to achieve ends, not for the ends themselves. Tacky, tasteless, sensationalistic, lurid, and exploitive—these are just a few of the adjectives used to describe his methods. However, his aim could always be described in one of the best-known of journalistic sayings: "It is the role of the press to comfort the afflicted and afflict the comfortable."

By 1897 Hearst had afflicted many of the money moguls and political fat cats. He had lost one major battle—he had thrown the support of his newspapers behind the presidential candidacy of William Jennings Bryan. Bryan had lost to William McKinley in the 1896 elections. Bryan was in favor of the income tax and for regulating the railroads and other major corporations. On these stands Hearst supported him, although Hearst disagreed with Bryan's support of unlimited coinage of silver, a platform known as "free silver."

Those who supported free silver believed the United States Treasury should be able to use silver to manufacture coins without restraint. Opposed to them were individuals, like Hearst, who believed that no coins should be minted without an equivalent supply of gold in the Treasury to back them up. The phrase "gold standard" represents the belief that all the money in circulation must be represented by real gold.

✳

"You furnish the pictures and I'll furnish the war."

Bryan's support of free silver split the Democratic party and caused Hearst considerable anguish. When he finally decided that his paper should support Bryan nevertheless, it was a courageous act. Hearst's decision was based on the belief that, aside from his flawed thinking about silver, Bryan was the best candidate for the people. Hearst's *New York Morning Journal* was the only newspaper in the East that supported Bryan, and its publisher was severely criticized for his stand.

If Bryan, and thus Hearst, lost the bid for the presidency, there were still other battles to wage. One was over the island of Cuba, which is 90 miles from the coast of Florida. The island was discovered by Christopher Columbus after his first voyage across the Atlantic Ocean, in 1492. Cuba was under Spanish rule. But following the examples of the United States and Mexico which had thrown off colonial rule, revolutionaries in Cuba were anxious to gain independence. It was a struggle Hearst could enter with unabated energy, a struggle that seemed as honorable as the American Revolution. Hearst threw his wholehearted support behind the Cuban rebels. All he needed was the right story.

Most of the news coming out of Cuba was biased and extremely unreliable. In Cuba, American reporters were confined to a hotel in the capital city of Havana, and their stories of Spanish atrocities against the rebels were vastly exaggerated, sometimes even completely fabricated.

In New York City, a political refugee by the name of Tomas Estrada Palma was the spokesman for revolutionary activity. He carried on intrigue and distributed information and propaganda about the Cuban Revolution. Palma used the office of an American lawyer sympathetic to the cause as his press headquarters. Every afternoon, reporters met there to hear the latest news, however trumped-up or exaggerated it may have been. Because a box of peanuts was always handy for a quick snack, the office came to be called the Peanut Club.

Hearst sent a two-man team to Cuba, writer Richard Harding Davis and artist Frederic Remington, whose paintings and bronze sculptures of the American West are famous. The two men checked into the Hotel Ingleterra with the other newsmen, but they found Havana to be peaceful.

"Everything is quiet. There is no trouble here. There will be no war. I wish to return," Remington cabled back to the newspaper after a time.

"Please remain. You furnish the pictures and I'll furnish the war," was Hearst's legendary reply.

Davis and Remington were responsible for one trumped-up story concerning three Cuban girls who, while traveling to the United States, were searched by a group of soldiers. "DOES OUR FLAG PROTECT WOMEN?" demanded a huge headline in the *Journal* on February 12, 1897. When the three young women arrived in New York, they denied that they had been undressed and searched by men, as the newspaper had claimed. Rather, they were searched by women while soldiers waited outside their stateroom.

The *World* delighted in the *Journal's* embarrassment, but that didn't stop Hearst.

On a hot day in August 1897, he came across a dispatch from Havana that propelled him on a new campaign. It read "Evangelina Cisneros, pretty girl of seventeen years, related to President of Cuban Republic, is to be imprisoned for twenty years on African coast for having taken part in uprising of Cuban political prisoners on Isle of Pines."

The facts were more subtle and complicated. Evangelina's father, an imprisoned revolutionary, had, in fact, been given a milder sentence after his daughter had argued on his behalf. Evangelina then had gone to the Isle of Pines, south of Cuba, where Señor Cisneros was imprisoned. She lured the Spanish colonel in charge of the prison to her cottage, where rebel sympathizers beat and tied him. But instead of succeeding in freeing her father, Evangelina was caught and sent to jail in Havana to await trial.

Hearst decided to make a national issue of the Cisneros case. More than 200 *Journal* contributors throughout the United States were asked to circulate petitions addressed to the Queen of Spain, asking for Evangelina's release. The contributors were told to get signatures of the most prominent women they could find, and they did. Among the 200,000 signers of the petitions were the mother of the president of the United States, the wife of the secretary of state, the widows of President Grant and Jefferson Davis, Clara Barton, the founder of the Red Cross, and Frances Hodgson Burnett, an author of children's books.

Meanwhile the *Journal* was plucking the national heartstrings in the most shameless manner: "The tenderly nurtured girl was imprisoned at eighteen among the most depraved . . . and now she is about to be sent in mockery to spend twenty years in a servitude that will kill her in a year." In fact, Evangelina Cisneros hadn't even been sentenced.

For two whole weeks the *Journal* relentlessly bombarded readers with grimy, greatly exaggerated, fabricated details until even the American consul general, General Fitzhugh Lee, denounced the sleazy sensationalism. ". . . I wish to correct a false and stupid impression which has been created by some newspapers. . . . This young woman had two clean rooms . . . and is well-clothed and fed. It is all tommy-rot about her scrubbing floors and being subjected to cruelties and indignities. She would have been pardoned long ago if it had not been for the hubbub created by American newspapers."

But that didn't stop the impresario of American journalism, who had little regard for truth when it got in the way of his causes or of winning the war he was waging against his competitor: Joseph Pulitzer and the *World*. He assigned one of his adventurer-reporters to go to Havana and get Evangelina out.

"EVANGELINA CISNEROS RESCUED BY THE *JOURNAL*—An American Newspaper Accomplishes at a Single Stroke What the Best Effort of Diplomacy Failed Utterly to Bring About in Many Months." Thus read the headline of the *Journal* on October 10, 1897. The story described in vivid terms how a disguised reporter had taken danger in stride and sawed through window bars to rescue her. He had then dressed Evangelina as a boy and smuggled her out of the country. Although the paper didn't mention this, the reporter had also bribed the jail guards so that they would look the other way while the rescue took place.

Possibly William Randolph Hearst really *did* believe in the "rightness" of the true romance rescue he had staged. Hearst liked to *believe* what his newspapers said about any situation, even though he *knew* that many of the stories in his papers did not tell the whole truth, only the truth as he perceived it.

The mysterious explosion of the U.S. battleship Maine *was used by Hearst and other newspaper publishers to whip up war hysteria.*

When the rescued heroine of this fantasy arrived in New York, she played her role to the hilt. She was given a suite of rooms in the new Waldorf Astoria hotel, regaled with flowers, dressed in lavish finery, and welcomed at a reception in Madison Square by 100,000 well-wishers. She was taken to Washington, D.C., to meet the president and was treated as if she were royalty. In truth, she was responsible for a criminal act and was still due to stand trial for her crime.

"The newspapers of your country seem to be more powerful than the government," was what the prime minister of Spain said to an American reporter.

Hearst still believed that war with Spain over Cuba was the correct position for the United States to assume. However, he hadn't been able to accomplish that action quite yet. Indeed, Spain was doing everything possible to avoid that war, including giving autonomy to Cuba, where the new government was beginning to establish reforms.

The decisive incident in this scenario occurred on February 15, 1898. The battleship U.S.S. *Maine*, stationed in Havana Harbor, mysteriously exploded, and 260 lives were lost. The *Journal* took the lead in declaring that the explosion was caused by Spanish mines, although there was no proof of that. It is possible the explosion was entirely accidental. If the explosion was indeed politically motivated, the Cuban rebels were likely responsible. They were still not in power and were more likely to profit by a war between Spain and the United States than was Spain.

The facts notwithstanding, fires were stoked by the "jingo journalism" of both Hearst's *Journal* and Pulitzer's *World*. They led other papers in pushing the country toward war with Spain, drowning out more restrained, sober voices. Finally, on April 19, 1898, Congress passed a joint resolution enabling the president to use armed forces in Cuba. The Spanish-American War had started.

Hearst was in the thick of things. He offered his yacht, the *Buccaneer*, to the government, and he chartered a British steamer and a fleet of tugs. With his staff of reporters, photographs, and artists on board, using a hand press, they published an edition of the *Journal*. Hearst sailed closer than advisable to the battle and went so far as to leap into the surf brandishing a huge revolver to capture a small party of stranded Spanish sailors.

The war lasted just a few months and ended with the Spanish giving up and leaving Cuba. American troops stayed on until the Republic of Cuba came into being in 1902.

The cause of the explosion of the battleship *Maine* remains a mystery to this day.

Cartoonist Thomas Nast compared Tammany boss William Marcy Tweed and a common thief in a sketch in Harper's Weekly *in 1872.*

Chapter 9

Power and Politics

*T*he war was over. William Randolph Hearst had been in the thick of it from the beginning, and he was heady with victory. Also, he could now boast that his newspaper, the *New York Morning Journal*, had the largest circulation of any paper in the world.

On September 25, 1898, Hearst took an unusual step—he published an impassioned editorial that said:

> The force of the newspaper is the greatest force in civilization.
>
> Under the republican government, newspapers form and express public opinion.
>
> They suggest and control legislation.
>
> They declare wars.
>
> They punish criminals, especially the powerful. They reward with approving publicity the good deeds of citizens everywhere.
>
> The newspapers control the nation because they

REPRESENT THE PEOPLE. . . .

I pledge the *Journal* to the support of all good measures proposed by other newspapers.

I urge upon the men whose power gives them such great responsibilities the importance of formal editorial union— not for private profit but FOR THE PUBLIC GOOD.

—W.R. Hearst

It was a stunning statement considering that, to the degree newspapers are "the greatest force in civilization," Hearst, as owner of the paper with the most readers, could be said to be in charge of this tremendous force. Theoretically, that would make him the most powerful man in the world, except, perhaps, for one individual: the president of the United States. Imagine, then, the omnipotence of the man, if the "lord of the press" were to become the most important elected official in the country as well.

Hearst's plea to other publishers was ignored. He never really understood that they were full of contempt for him and his ruthless methods of manipulating the news. It was never totally clear whether he was motivated by his ideals and principles or by his drive to increase the circulation of his publications. The two purposes were probably so closely entwined that Hearst could not distinguish them from each other.

Although his colleagues in the publishing world ignored Hearst's plea for cooperation, they would soon be paying attention to him. Although they probably wished that his name would simply vanish, they would find, instead, that their papers were forced to print it on a rather regular basis. William Randolph Hearst soon set off in pursuit of the only position of power that could be considered equal to the one he already held—he began his quest for the presidency of the United States.

Consider the courage this decision took. Remember, Hearst was so shy that his shyness was nearly paralyzing. He hated shaking hands and, when he did so, his handshake was a limp, unwelcome gesture. Also his voice was so soft and weak, it was difficult to hear. Yet, as a political candidate, Hearst would be forced to meet multitudes of new people. He would have to get accustomed to glad-handing and public speaking and facing enormous crowds. And he was willing to overcome all of these obstacles to achieve his overriding goal.

In addition to those personally difficult self-disciplines, Hearst would have to compromise his integrity. For one thing, he would have to make peace with the most scandalous American political organization in history, Tammany Hall. Tammany Hall was unique among the country's local political clubs. Through these clubs, which usually had meeting places where social functions were held, political patronage was handed out.

The New York City club began as the Sons of St. Tammany. Tammany was an Indian chief famous for his kindness and love of liberty. Calling him "saint" was meant to ridicule British Tory organizations that used names like St. George and St. David. Officially called the Society of St. Tammany, or Columbian Order, members had supported American independence. In the early days, membership in the club was not dependent on membership in a political party. Rather, it was a charitable organization. In the nineteenth century, Tammany Hall moved toward political activity, naming and supporting candidates. In 1846 the notorious William M. "Boss" Tweed was head of the club. He and his confederates were so unscrupulous in taking bribes and in making deals that Tammany Hall became known throughout the world as the symbol of corrupt politics.

Hearst scorned the activities of Tammany, yet he found himself courting its members, especially the current boss, Richard Crocker, who had once been accused of murder. Hearst first got inside Tammany by attending a fund-raising event at the club's headquarters in Union Square in the spring of 1899.

Hearst's political ambitions were set aside for a time while he took another trip abroad. His guests this time included the Willson family: parents and two daughters. One of the daughters, Millicent, was to become Mrs. William Randolph Hearst.

During this trip while on a cruise along the Nile river in Egypt, Hearst was reading a two-week-old English newspaper. He learned that the United States and Great Britain were about to sign a treaty to give the United States control over the Panama Canal, which was about to be built. The Panama Canal was to be a 51-mile-long waterway through the strip of land connecting North and South America and separating the Caribbean Sea and the Pacific Ocean. It would be American-financed and American-built. The treaty included the provision that the Canal would not be fortified. Hearst was outraged.

He wired his papers, ordering them to protest. Following the chief's orders, Hearst's lieutenants rushed their protests to Washington, D.C., and into print. In the end, the treaty was defeated. When canal construction was finished in 1914 it was fortified, a caution that proved very useful when World War I broke out in that same year.

Certainly Hearst's activities showed how thoroughly he believed in his role as watchdog of the American nation. As he himself had written, it was of vital importance for him, through the newspapers, to "suggest and control legislation." Without doubt, the Democrats saw how important Hearst's newspapers could be for the party.

When the National Association of Democratic Clubs met in Washington, D.C., on May 19, 1900, William Randolph Hearst was there. He was told that the Democratic party badly needed a newspaper to represent its interests in the Chicago area. In record time, six weeks, Hearst launched the *Chicago American*. Ordinarily such a start-up would take many months. In return for his willingness to launch a new newspaper in Chicago, Hearst was nominated, and

elected, to the post of president of the Association. It was his first serious step into organized politics.

Hearst and his crew got the *Chicago American* rolling in time for the Democratic national convention, which began in Kansas City on July 4. William Jennings Bryan, whom Hearst had supported in 1896, was again nominated to run for the presidency. If Hearst had hoped to be named vice president, he was disappointed. He remained independent of the party to the extent that he opposed two of its plat-

The headquarters of Tammany Hall were on 14th Street in New York City.

form positions: to attack Republican-backed imperialism (Hearst favored American conquest as avidly as Theodore Roosevelt did) and to support free silver (the same Bryan platform Hearst had opposed during Bryan's first, unsuccessful run for the office). Hearst joined the Democrats wholeheartedly in their third platform, which was to take control of the trusts that ran roughshod over the nation.

The name "trusts" is ironic considering the role they played. Trusts were business firms, or corporations, that banded together to control prices and reduce outside competition from other businesses. The oil trust or the railroad trust could dictate such things as price, quality, distribution, and availability. In addition, they used their vast financial resources and power to buy governmental favor. The Sherman Antitrust Act of 1890 had been passed in an effort to curb the activities of trusts. However, this act lacked teeth, and the trusts and corporations found legal ways to get around it. Trusts were, in fact, getting larger and larger, controlling the prices of hundreds of necessary commodities, ranging from coal and steel to whiskey and coffins. Hearst and his press had been battling the trusts long and hard.

Hearst did not run for national office in 1900, but his political career was launched. At a dinner party he sat at the head of the table, between the presidential candidate and his wife, and afterward he went over to Madison Square Garden, where a major celebration with fireworks was to take place.

"The huge Garden was packed with enthusiastic Democrats," wrote W.A. Swanberg in his biography of William Randolph Hearst. "Hearst, clad in evening dress, had to pound for order for ten minutes," the *Times* said, "laughing outright when some individual in the crowd yelled, 'Three Cheers for Willie Hearst.' Then he simply announced that the meeting was in order and introduced Anson Phelps Stokes as permanent chairman. This brief moment of leadership was fated to enslave him like a drug."

Chapter 10

Trouble Hounds Hearst

*T*wice William Randolph Hearst backed William Jennings Bryan's quest for the presidency, and two times Bryan lost to William McKinley. After the second time, in 1900, Hearst was prepared to learn by past mistakes and look ahead to 1904. Then, an unpredictable series of events thrust Hearst into the center of a devastating and long-lasting controversy.

President William McKinley gave a speech at the Pan-American Exposition in Buffalo, New York, on September 5, 1901. After the speech, hundreds of citizens filed by to pay their respects. One of them, Leon Czolgosz, carried a concealed gun, which was hidden under a handkerchief. As Czolgosz stepped up to the president, he revealed the gun and shot McKinley twice. McKinley died nine days later.

In the minds of many people, William Randolph Hearst deserved a large share of the responsibility for McKinley's death, because of two separate items that had appeared in his papers. The first was a foolish bit of verse written by Ambrose Bierce, a man with a caustic wit whom Hearst had hired when he took over the *San Francisco Examiner*. Bierce was writing about William Goebel, governor-elect of Kentucky, who had just been shot to death in an election quarrel:

> *The bullet that pierced Goebel's breast*
> *Cannot be found in all the West*
> *Good reason, it is speeding here*
> *To stretch McKinley on his bier.*

These words had appeared in the *New York Morning Journal* on February 4, 1900, more than a year before McKinley's assassination, but they came back to haunt Hearst. So, too, did an editorial comment written by Arthur Brisbane, one of Hearst's top employees and a good friend. Some time earlier Brisbane had written so viciously about McKinley that Hearst had felt it necessary to apologize to the president. Then, on April 10, 1901, five months before McKinley was shot, an unsigned editorial appeared in the *Journal*. The editorial, written by Brisbane, said: "If bad institutions and bad men can be rid of only by killing, then the killing must be done."

Those words were totally irresponsible under any circumstances. In fact, when Hearst learned of the comment, he had the presses stopped and the content changed. Thus, that sentiment appeared only in the earlier editions of the paper. Following McKinley's assassination in September, the words proved to be worse than irresponsible; they were considered incendiary.

Turning on Hearst, his enemies in the press reprinted the editorial and the verse, as well as the various anti-McKinley cartoons that had appeared in Hearst papers. They even fabricated a report that the murderer had a copy of Hearst's paper in his pocket when he was arrested. In truth, the man never even read the Hearst paper.

Across the country Hearst was hanged in effigy. Passersby often threw stones and cursed the man whom they blamed for President McKinley's death. Ambrose Bierce later explained that the purpose of his verse was to warn of the danger that would ensue if Goebel's assassins were not captured and punished. He said, moreover, that Hearst was entirely unaware of the verse's publication. However, widespread anger and outright hatred was directed towards the publisher. Many households and organizations refused to allow a Hearst publication on their premises, and in some places Hearst papers were seized and burned.

Hearst remained aloof from the controversy for the most part, although he did write one editorial stating that the only offense of his papers was that "they fought for the people, and against privilege and class pride and class greed and class stupidity and class heartlessness with more daring weapons, with more force and talent and enthusiasm than any other newspapers in the country."

Sometime after his apologetic explanation of the meaning of his printed words, Bierce said, "Hearst's newspapers . . . had been incredibly rancorous toward McKinley, but no doubt it was my luckless prophesy that cost (Hearst) tens of thousands of dollars and a growing political prestige. . . . I have never mentioned the matter to him, nor . . . has he ever mentioned it to me."

Despite the scalding accusations and with the support of Tammany politicos, Hearst became a candidate for a congressional seat from New York's 11th District in October 1902. The new Tammany boss was Charles Francis Murphy, who took over from Crocker. Murphy knew how much the party needed the support of Hearst's newspapers and backed the publisher's candidacy. The 11th District was a heavily Democratic district, and victory was pretty much assured. Nevertheless Hearst campaigned vigorously and planned a huge rally in Madison Square

※
Many households and organizations refused to allow a Hearst publication on their premises, and in some places Hearst papers were seized and burned.

Garden. The celebration was electrically lighted with the words "Congress Must Control the Trusts." These words were the motto that was printed every day in his morning newspaper, the *New York American*. Elaborate fireworks, bands, banners, and parades enlivened the celebration.

Ten thousand people waving American flags cheered that night. Hearst talked to them about the privileges that the trusts had enjoyed under the Republican party, and the privileges that the party had, in turn, received from the trusts. "You cannot stick a pin in the trusts without hearing a shriek from the Republican party; and you cannot stick a pin in the Republican party without hearing a roar from the trusts," he told the crowd.

Because his voice was so soft, most people could not hear him, but they were in sympathy with his point of view and applauded when those within earshot did so. One man in the the audience made everyone laugh when he shouted in booming, resonant tones, "Oh, how I wish you had my voice."

Another Hearst extravaganza was planned for Madison Square Garden on election night. Hearst easily won the post, but his victory was not without pain. One of the fireworks ignited prematurely and set off explosions in a pile of bombs. It was like a battle scene, with windows shattering and glass falling. Eighteen people died and as many as 100 were injured. Because of this tragic accident, some of Hearst's pleasure in his victory was spoiled for a long time afterward.

Chapter *11*

Husband, Father, Presidential Hopeful

"*M*y mother was against it," Millicent Hearst told a reporter, many years later about her first date with William Randolph Hearst. It was 1897 and she was Millicent Veronica Willson, a beautiful sixteen-year-old dancer in a Broadway show called "The Girl from Paris." She didn't know who the polite, well-dressed stranger was when he appeared backstage at the theater and asked her to go out with him.

"We were carefully supervised in those days and I recall (mother) said, 'Who is he? Some young fellow from out West somewhere, isn't he?' She insisted (my sister) Anita come or I couldn't go. Well, he took us down to the *Journal*—the *New York Morning Journal*—we'd hardly heard of it, and he showed us over it, all over it. I hadn't the foggiest notion what we were doing, walking miles on rough boards in thin, high-heeled evening slippers, and I thought my feet would kill me. Of course this wasn't our idea of a good time. . . . Anita kept whispering to me, 'We're going to get thrown out of here Milly, the way he behaves you'd think he owned it.' It wasn't until our next trip that I found out he did."

Perhaps the story is embellished—Hearst was quite well known as a man-about-town by that time, and he loved going to the theater. Hearst courted Millicent Willson for several years, and often escorted both sisters on their evenings out. He had taken the entire Willson family abroad in 1899, but the marriage didn't take place until April 28, 1903.

The ceremony took place at Grace Church, in New York City. The alter was lavishly decorated with roses, but the wedding was a relatively quiet affair for a man given to the kind of fireworks and extravaganzas Hearst liked to stage. He even made reporters and photographers from his own newspapers wait outside the church, and when he and Millicent emerged from the church, they didn't stop to be interviewed or have pictures taken. Instead they hurried into their carriage and rode away. Although the marriage of a celebrity like Hearst could very well be carried on the front page, it was tucked away in the back of his own papers. That was, without doubt, in accordance with his wishes. There was a wedding breakfast at the Waldorf Astoria hotel and then, in the afternoon, the Hearsts boarded a ship for a honeymoon in Europe.

Phoebe Hearst, who had tried to discourage William from his interest in people of the theater, was unable to attend the ceremony. She sent Millicent a set of emeralds as a wedding gift. When the couple returned from Europe, they took a tour of Hearst properties in Mexico and then visited Phoebe Hearst in California. Although Phoebe Hearst was originally cool toward the idea of her son marrying a showgirl, she and Millicent later became good friends.

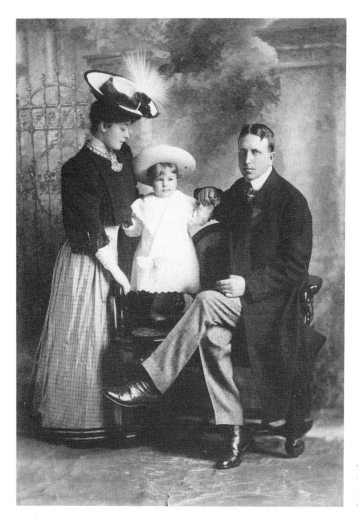

Millicent and William Randolph Hearst with their oldest son, George, born in 1904.

While he was in London on his honeymoon, Hearst read a copy of a new British magazine called *The Car*. He sent a message to one of his managers in New York giving instructions that a similar Hearst publication should be launched. Thus he began his foray into the magazine field with a venture called *Motor*.

William and Millicent's first son, George Randolph, was born on April 10, 1904, and William became a doting father. A story is told that, while a heat wave plagued the city during the baby's first summer, Hearst raced around bringing in fans and buckets of ice to devise a kind of improvised air-conditioning system for the baby. The Hearst family would eventually include five sons.

By this time Hearst had begun his term in Congress, and he didn't waste any time in alienating some powerful Democrats. Instead of keeping a low profile and playing his cards carefully, as most freshman representatives would, he began by pushing his weight around to secure a position on the House Labor Committee.

Hearst knew the programs he wanted passed and he was impatient. He was still after the trusts, which he was anxious and determined to see brought under stern controls. He believed that the government, not private individuals, should own the railroads, telegraph lines, and perhaps even mines. He also promoted the idea of an eight-hour workday. He was in favor of the graduated income tax and favored direct, popular election of United States senators, rather than election by the state legislatures, as was then the system. Popular election, he believed, would make senators more responsible to the public and less beholden to big business interests. He was in favor of expanding the military and, showing his mother's influence, he was ardent in his support of public education.

Hearst did not personally present all his proposals to the legislature. Rather, he mobilized a group of about six or seven representatives, known as the "Hearst Brigade," who introduced legislative proposals on his behalf. Not many of his measures were passed.

Sitting and listening, and making speeches, was not his style, so Hearst was not often to be found attending legislative sessions. He had a great many detractors, who commented on everything from his absences at roll call to the vulgarity of his newspapers. The complaints were especially energetic, because it was increasingly clear to all that Hearst had his eye on the presidency. Personal dislike of Hearst may have blinded some to the positive side of his programs. Many still blamed him for McKinley's death.

Although he was having difficulty building a broad base of support, Hearst was expanding his newspaper empire. In 1903, he started paper number seven, the *Los Angeles Examiner*. The *Boston American*, paper number eight, began publication in 1904. According to some reports, he sent word to his editors to tone language down a bit in view of his possible candidacy for the highest office in the land.

Hearst was traveling and campaigning and gaining some strength in the West. He won the state convention in Iowa, but lost to his opponent, Judge Alton B. Parker, at the Indiana convention. He was working his way toward the national convention, which would be held in St. Louis in July 1904.

The outstanding question was whether Bryan, whom Hearst had twice backed, would throw his weight behind the publisher. The answer, it turned out, was no. Bryan nominated a senator from Missouri. Hearst was nominated by a Californian who had been a colleague of his father. As the balloting went on, Hearst got 263 votes, but Parker, who was named later in the convention, secured the Democrat presidential nomination with 658 votes.

ONLY A STEPPING-STONE

Hearst's political ambitions were caricatured in Harper's Magazine *in 1906.*

Chapter 12

Fighting Back

When scoundrels, or those considered to be scoundrels, came under attack in newspapers belonging to William Randolph Hearst, there were no holds barred. Hearst could hand criticism out, but how did he react when it was directed at him?

Usually he brushed it off with an amused smile. After McKinley's assassination, when the fiercest accusations came his way, he resorted only to a modest defense of his newspapers' policies. Even his greatest detractors admitted that he had conducted himself with restraint.

However, Hearst did know how to fight back, as he proved during the third session of the Fifty-eighth Congress, which ran from December 5, 1904, to March 4, 1905. Congressman Hearst had sponsored a bill to bring the railroads under tighter control by the government. When the bill came up before the House for consideration, he was not present. A representative from Massachusetts, Democrat John A. Sullivan, took advantage of the chance to needle Hearst for neglecting legislative sessions, especially when his bill came up and needed some explanation. Hearst's New York paper shot back at Sullivan, calling him a "bald, red-nosed young man who had revealed his unsuspected presence in the House of Representatives by asking some questions which showed that he knew nothing of the hearings before various committees on railway legislation."

On February 13, rising to retaliate, Sullivan called Hearst "a swaggering bully" with a "political assassination department." When a point of order was made on the ground that Sullivan was speaking against the motives of a fellow member of the House, the speaker, a Republican who was enjoying this tussle between Democrats, let the attack continue. He said that Sullivan was talking "not (about) a member of the House but a newspaperman." This ruling was received with laughter, sniping, jeers, and a general uproar.

Sullivan continued: "Many members of this House must feel some curiosity to know why the gentleman from New York ever breaks his custom by coming into the House at all. He comes here solely because the position offers him an opportunity to exploit his candidacy for the presidency of the United States." Sullivan further targeted Hearst's presidential aspirations, saying that the Democratic party had once before nominated an editor "but . . . had never nominated a mere checkbook." Sullivan went on to enter into the Congressional Record a nasty attack that called Hearst a liar, blackmailer, and bribe-taker.

The chaos and applause that followed Sullivan's remarks revealed how much Hearst was hated by many of his cohorts. Though he must have been livid with rage, he rose and spoke calmly in his soft, high voice. Unlike his colleagues, who regularly attended legislative sessions to fill the record with their meaningless and ineffective "chewed wind," Hearst claimed that his attendance was based on what he considered the best interests of the people he represented. "And," he went on, "I have heard the best speakers deliver the most admirable addresses on the floor of this House without influencing legislation in the slightest particular." At that Hearst received applause.

Then Hearst dropped his own bombshell. "When I was at Harvard College in 1885, a murder was committed in a low saloon in Cambridge. A man partly incapacitated from drink bought in that saloon on Sunday morning, when the saloon was open against the law, was assaulted by the two owners of that saloon and brutally kicked to death. The name of one of the owners of that saloon was John A. Sullivan, and these two men were arrested and indicted by the grand jury for manslaughter and tried and convicted. I would like to ask the gentleman from Massachusetts if he knows anything about that incident, and whether, if I desired to make a hostile criticism, I could not have referred to that crime?"

The scene in the House was one of pandemonium. Hearst had accused a fellow member of Congress of murder. He said he regretted the necessity of doing so, but insisted, "I must describe and define the character of the men who attack me. It is the duty of a newspaper when such men are found in public life to call attention to them. I have incurred the hostility of this class of men and it shall be my pride and joy to continue to deserve it so long as I remain in journalism or in Congress."

As the facts of the case revealed, John A. Sullivan was a boy of 17 at the time of the incident in the saloon. The "other person" was his father, the owner of the saloon. The person ejected from the saloon had fallen on the sidewalk and cracked his skull. Sullivan later explained to the House that his father had been pardoned after serving 18 months of his three-year sentence and that he, himself, had been put on probation.

William Randolph Hearst was convinced that Sullivan and other members of his party were scheming to discredit him. Hearst meant to show them that they were treading on dangerous ground when they took him on. He could set off verbal fireworks that burst as effectively as the visibly explosive kind.

The split with his own Democratic party was widened over the next couple of years, when Hearst broke away from Tammany and its then current boss Charles F. Murphy. In 1905, Hearst joined forces with a third party: the Municipal Ownership League. The League wanted Hearst to run for mayor of New York City on their ticket. Hearst was reluctant, at first, probably because he preferred the post of governor as a stepping stone to the presidency. In a letter to the head of the League, Hearst wrote, "I do not think it would be in the best interest of the independent movement (for me to) to become its leader." He mentioned the powerful and vindictive enemies he had made "through my endeavors to overthrow special privilege and corruption in high places. . . . I am proud of my friends . . . and I am almost equally proud of my enemies, for these belong to the rich, powerful, and unscrupulous class that most people are afraid to have as enemies.

❋
"Oh, I am just looking for a coffin for Tammany."

"I am NOT afraid of them. I glory in doing battle with them whenever I see their greedy hands outstretched for the public purse. But I AM afraid to array their power and wealth and unscrupulous methods in their most violent form against a movement which means so much for the welfare of the community."

Despite his protests, members of the Municipal Ownership League continued trying to persuade Hearst to run. When he mounted the platform during their convention, the crowd cheered and hailed him for a full seven minutes, and ended up nominating him for mayor. A few days later he accepted the nomination because, as he wrote, "The situation in this city is so grave and the condition of the public in the face of organized bossism is apparently so helpless that no man has a right to consider anything else, least of all his private affairs or personal inclination."

Hearst's candidacy in 1905 was a crusade for good government. He also wanted the city to own utilities like the railways, which at that time ran along the city streets. He promised new schools and better wages and improved working conditions for city employees.

On election day, Hearst went out to vote before breakfast. He left home alone, but before he had gone very far a crowd of supporters surrounded him, cheering and wishing him well. The polling place was in a funeral parlor, and he joked with members of his entourage saying, "Oh, I am just looking for a coffin for Tammany."

He seemed certain to be the people's choice. He was greeted with wild enthusiasm wherever he went, and it appeared that he would win the election and dismantle the corrupt political machine. It looked as though William Randolph Hearst was about to accomplish the astounding feat of bringing Tammany to its knees.

But the power of the machine won out in an election that was as crooked as ever. Votes were bought and counted twice; Hearst workers and poll watchers were offered bribes. Those who would not accept bribes were beaten up and forced to leave their posts. Some of them, bleeding, straggled in to Hearst's elegant Lexington Avenue home, which was crowded with antiques and works of art. The candidate, who had been playing with his year-old son, remained calm. "Let's fix these men up and put others in their place."

Gangs of Tammany repeaters—as those who voted several times were called—and roughnecks marched from one polling place to the next, creating havoc and getting away with it. Entire ballot boxes containing votes for Hearst were thrown into the East River. The results of the vote count showed that Hearst had lost by about 3,500 votes—a negligible number. If the voting had been honest, he likely would have won by a substantial majority, as many as 50,000 votes. He declared: "We have won this election. All Tammany's frauds, all Tammany's false registration, illegal voting, and dishonest counting have not been able to overcome the great popular majority. The recount will show that we won the election by many thousands of votes. I shall fight this battle to the end, in behalf of the people who cast their votes for me, and who shall not be disenfranchised by any effort of the criminal bosses."

Hearst's papers screamed fraud. On November 10, 1905, the headline of the *New York Morning Journal* read: "LOOK OUT MURPHY! It's A Short Lockstep From Delmonico's (a fancy restaurant) to Sing Sing (the federal penitentiary)."

The same edition carried a cartoon of the rotund Boss Murphy dressed in a striped prison uniform. "Every honest voter of New York WANTS TO SEE YOU IN THIS COSTUME," read the caption under the cartoon.

Murphy was never even taken to court, however. There was a recount, but it proved nothing, since most of cheating had taken place outside the polling places, before ballots were cast. An investigation revealed numerous instances of illegal voting, strong-arming, and fraud. It led to election reforms, but did not make Hearst mayor of New York City.

Hearst's campaign for mayor had threatened the hold Tammany Hall had on New York City. His defeat had been costly and dangerous, but the Tammany bosses knew Hearst would destroy them and their machine if he wasn't stopped.

Chapter *13*

Still Fighting

*S*an Francisco was first settled by the Spanish in 1776 as a fort and mission on the northern coast of the city. The gold rush that began in 1848 and brought George Hearst to the West Coast also brought gambling and violence, along with tremendous wealth. San Francisco grew quickly after 1860, and by 1900 was the tenth largest city in the country.

Disaster struck in April 1906. An earthquake and an ensuing fire that lasted three days ravaged San Francisco, destroying almost 500 city blocks. Fully two-thirds of the city smouldered in ruin.

Hearst was notified of the earthquake early on the morning of April 18. He was awakened from his sleep by a phone call, but was unperturbed at the news of the earthquake. "They have earthquakes often," he said.

The gravity of the situation was revealed during the day. Among the ruins were the buildings and

Armed troops patrol Market Street in San Francisco to prevent looting after the 1906 earthquake.

plant of the *San Francisco Examiner* worth $2 million. His mother's townhouse and art collection also were destroyed.

Hearst swung into action and the *Examiner* didn't miss an issue. First it was combined with two other San Francisco papers. Within a week the publisher had bought, at double its price, new machinery that was on its way to a newspaper in Salt Lake City. He had the railroad cars in which the press was being shipped to Utah attached, instead, to an express train en route to San Francisco. Soon, the *Examiner* was back in business in a newer and bigger building.

Besides restoring the *Examiner,* Hearst also organized fund-raising benefits, charity bazaars, and theatrical benefits. He went to Washington, D.C., to introduce a bill appropriating $4.5 million to rebuild public structures. He sponsored and publicized relief trains that departed from Los Angeles, Chicago, and New York. When he went to San Francisco in person, he carried with him $200,000 that had been raised through his newspapers.

"Almost overpowered by the desert of tumbled brick, tangled iron, and blackened timbers, Hearst wandered to the district . . . in which he had played as a boy," wrote Mrs. Fremont Older, of Hearst's visit to the devastated city. "He was relieved to find that the ancient Mission Dolores was spared. Then he went northward to the bay to see what had survived of his childhood home. Strangely enough, his hillside home and that delightful sunny nook of San Francisco lay smiling in the sunshine, wholly unconscious of the city's disaster."

Back in the business district, the scene was dreadful. "Women and children were huddled in tents (set up) in little parks that had shriveled in the flames. Portsmouth Square, where the American flag had first flown in San Francisco, was crowded with refugees—laughing, singing refugees, already dreaming of another splendid (rebuilt) city with a splendid future." The city was under martial law, but overwhelming as was the calamity, Hearst rejoiced that the people were not overwhelmed or discouraged. He wrote, "Everything has been destroyed except that indomitable American pluck, that unconquerable American spirit which will not be subdued. The past is already forgotten, the future is in everyone's mind."

As for Hearst's political setback, his striking loss of mayoralty, he put that in the past tense, too. Back in New York, he returned his attentions to crusading against graft and defending the underprivileged. And he became a candidate for governor of the state of New York.

The Municipal Ownership League, the party for which he had run for mayor, had become the Independence League and was fully expecting Hearst to be its gubernatorial candidate. It was, in fact, extending its range to include more national influence, in anticipation of trying for the presidency in 1908.

Boss Murphy of Tammany was worried. The man whom Hearst's papers had put into prison stripes was now taking tentative steps toward Hearst. The publisher seemed to be resisting the overtures. Then, a bizarre turn of events took place at the Democratic convention, which was held in Buffalo, New York, on September 27, 1906. Murphy actually negotiated with convention delegates to the point where he got them to nominate William Randolph Hearst, his mortal enemy, as the party's candidate for governor.

The rationale for this merger was a common belief that a fusion of the Independence League with the Democratic party would assure victory. Hearst could continue to insist that he still disapproved of Murphy and the machine, while taking advantage of the votes that the collaboration would bring him.

Running against Hearst on the Republican ticket was Charles Evans Hughes, an attorney who had earlier won Hearst's admiration for his work investigating corrupt political connections in the large insurance companies. Now Hearst described Hughes, his opponent, as an "animated feather duster."

Hughes then accused Hearst, who was the self-proclaimed "enemy of corporations," of being one of the country's biggest capitalists, whose publishing and real estate ventures were part of a complex web of corporate holdings. It was charged that Hearst avoided paying taxes, and that the "champion of labor" and advocate of the eight-hour day employed miners who slaved under terrible conditions for ten hours a day.

The most serious blow to Hearst's candidacy came when President Theodore Roosevelt sent his secretary of state, Elihu Root, to New York to campaign against Hearst. Everyone who was against Hearst, including the Republican president, feared that if Hearst was elected governor, he would be the presidential candidate in 1908.

Once again, the death of President McKinley was held up and used against Hearst. The words of now President Roosevelt, spoken years earlier against Hearst, were repeated by Root, who added, "I say, by the president's authority, that in penning these words, with the horror of President McKinley's murder fresh before him, he had Mr. Hearst specifically in mind. And I say, by his authority, that what he thought of Mr. Hearst then he thinks of Mr. Hearst now."

This speech delivered in the last days of the campaign, had its intended effect. The voice of the president resonated through the state of New York, and the wave of popularity that Hearst had been riding broke before he reached the top. He lost his bid for the governorship and the opportunity to run for president all at once.

Chapter 14

The
Muckrakers

At the turn of the century, newspaper campaigns for reform were joined by a type of magazine crusading that would come to be called "muckraking." The magazines were less sensational than the yellow press, and the most respected among them were more measured and more thoroughly documented. These magazines exposed all kinds of illegal and dangerous practices, from using poisons and alcohol in patent medicines to the corruption of government officials by business tycoons.

The greatest muckraking magazine was *McClure's,* and the best known of its contributors was a woman named Ida Tarbell. In fact, during the early part of the twentieth century Ida Tarbell was the most famous woman in the United States. Over a period of about four years, she worked on a history of the Standard Oil Company and a biography of its owner, John D. Rockefeller. She scrupulously documented the undercover deals, the graft, and the dishonesty and cruelty with which Rockefeller and his associates cheated their competitors and the public. Tarbell's efforts, aided by the efforts of Hearst and others, finally led to a Supreme Court decision calling for an end to the Standard Oil monopoly.

Another of the first-rank muckrakers, also writing for *McClure's* at the time, was Lincoln Steffens, who wrote exposés of the criminal behavior of politicians in a number of American cities. In 1906, Tarbell and Steffens and a few of their colleagues left *McClure's* and started their own publication, *The American Magazine*. In November 1906 *The American Magazine* published an article titled "Hearst, The Man Of Mystery," which came out while Hearst was campaigning for governor of New York.

Steffens' colleagues were all interested in what he was writing about Hearst. "I soon realized that they expected me to expose Hearst and the Hearst papers as I had the worst bosses and the worst cities," wrote Steffens in his autobiography. "And I had no such intention. Hearst, in journalism, was like a reformer in politics; he was an innovator who was crashing into the business, upsetting the order of things, and he was not doing it as we would have had it done. He was doing it his way."

His fellow journalists, said Steffens, "wished that someone would come along with money and brains enough to make a newspaper which they could all read, and perhaps write for, happily. But Hearst—he, with his millions, was making a paper that nobody liked; 'everybody' loathed his sheets in every city where he had one. We forbade it in our clubs; we wouldn't be seen with it, except here and there one of us would 'fall for the money' and write for it. . . . I cannot describe the hate in those days for Hearst."

Steffens was unwilling to pander to that hatred, and he argued with his colleagues on the editorial

Lincoln Steffens (1866–1936) was managing editor of McClure's *magazine before he became the first of the muckrakers.*

board of *The American Magazine* about the way in which he would portray Hearst. In the end he compromised somewhat. Steffens believed that Hearst did have certain virtues, and these and his money helped Hearst to get around red tape and other delaying methods. He worked for democracy as he saw it, in his own way, determined not to pander to others' beliefs. It was a manner that he had developed over the years with some success. A word portrait of Hearst by Steffens incorporates these characteristics:

"He is a tall man who does not strike you as tall. . . . He doesn't assert his strength either. Well built, and well groomed, he is strong physically, yet you get no sense of physical force. He never throws his chest out or his shoulders back. He uses his physical strength only for endurance. He is one of those tireless workers who work with the body at ease. . . . All is repose. Nothing is asserted, not even his authority. His orders to his editors go to them as suggestions and queries.

"Everything about Mr. Hearst is elusive. His blond hair is browning; his blue eyes are grayish; his clean-shaven face is smooth; his low voice speaks reluctantly and little, and then very slowly . . . you begin to notice that his straight, strong nose strikes straight down from his forehead; his straight mouth is thin-lipped and hard; and his eyes, cold, sharp, and curiously close together, can look straight into yours. A smile blurs these features at first, a sober smile which disarms without winning you."

In 1905, Hearst bought *Cosmopolitan* magazine. He already owned *Motor* magazine and several newspapers, but he was ready to move into the very different world of magazine publishing. Magazines had undergone revolutionary changes during the last decades of the nineteenth century and the beginning of the twentieth. Prices had been lowered, so ordinary people could afford to read them and, of course, more people were learning to read. Mailing costs were becoming less expensive, and an effort was made to appeal to popular taste as well as that of the intellectual minority. Advances in printing, which included printing illustrations, along with the establishment of railroads, contributed to the increasing mass circulation of magazines. By the year 1900, there were 50 national magazines, *Scientific American*, *National Geographic*, and *Harper's Weekly* among them.

Cosmopolitan had been launched in 1886, and by the end of 1892 it was among the country's leading illustrated magazines. But its editor and publisher, John Brisben Walker, bought the Stanley Automobile Company. He became so involved with the new technology of automobile manufacturing that, in 1905, he sold the magazine to Hearst for $400,000.

In 1906 Hearst's *Cosmopolitan* published a new series of articles that shook the foundations of the United States legislative body. Research for this series was done by Gustavus Myers, and the articles were written by David Graham Phillips. The title of the series was "The Treason of the Senate," and the first installment set the tone: "The senators are not elected by the people: they are elected by the 'interests' [and these are] as hostile to the American people as any invading army."

The theme was familiar to followers of Hearst, for he had been arguing that the senate was corrupt for years. The magazine made clear that this series was to be the most sensational, the most important, example of crusading journalism to date, "the most conspicuous act of exposure of corruption" ever attempted.

Hearst was in Washington, D.C., when the first article in the series which attacked New York Senator Chauncey M. Depew, was about to appear, and he read an early version. He sent it back with requests that more facts be added to the mix. "I had intended an exposé," he telegraphed the magazine office. "We have merely an attack. The facts, the proof, the documentary evidence are an important thing, but the article is deficient in them."

The presses were stopped and a number of facts inserted. These facts included documentation from Senate hearings that Senator Depew had an annual retainer of $20,000 from the Equitable Life Assurance Company. It was the publication of this very series that led President Theodore Roosevelt to label these exposes as "muckraking." The name caught on then and is used to this day to describe investigative journalism that uncovers wrongdoing, especially on the part of politicians and business executives. Roosevelt took the phrase from John Bunyan's book, *Pilgrim's Progress* where it was used to describe the man with the rake who fixed his eyes on cleaning the mire on the ground instead of looking up to the heavens.

Ida Tarbell (1857–1944), the author of The History of the Standard Oil Company, *which exposed its ruthless business practices and misuse of natural resources, also worked for* McClure's *and* The American Magazine.

"There are beautiful things above and around them (the muckrakers)," President Roosevelt insisted, "and if they gradually grow to feel that the whole world is nothing but muck, their power of usefulness is gone. If the whole picture is painted black there remains no hue whereby to single out the rascals for distinction from their fellows."

Nevertheless, it was *Cosmopolitan's* carefully documented series on the Senate that substantially contributed to the passage, six years later, of the 17th Amendment to the Constitution of the United States. That Amendment provides for the direct, popular election of senators to the U.S. Congress.

If the *Cosmopolitan* series set off sparks, so did another of Hearst's revelations that came two years later during the campaigns for the presidential election. Though Hearst himself was not running for office, he was campaigning vigorously for the candidates put forward by the Independence League. On the night of September 15, during a speech in Columbus, Ohio, Hearst ignited a string of fireworks that stunned the country. He began to read aloud from some letters that had been taken from the files of John D. Archbold, the vice president of Standard

Oil Company. It was a Hearst exclusive. He had bought the letters, which were obtained illegally, three years earlier. He had held on to them until what he believed to be the opportune moment. He chose the moment when the presidential campaigns were heating up. These incredibly incriminating letters revealed the extent to which this company bought the favors of senators and congressmen. They revealed misconduct of Democrats and Republicans alike.

"I am not here with empty assertions, but with legal evidence and documentary proof," Hearst told his audience. "I am now going to read copies of letters written by Mr. John Archbold, chief agent of Standard Oil, an intimate personal representative of Mr. Rockefeller . . ."

Among the letters he read were these:

"Dear Senator: In accordance with our understanding, I now beg to enclose . . . a certificate of deposit to your favor for $15,000. . . ." And, "My Dear Senator: Here is still another very objectionable bill. It is so outrageous as to be ridiculous, but it needs to be looked after, and I hope there will be no difficulty in killing it." Then, "My Dear Senator: I enclose your certificate of deposit to your favor for $15,000. . . . I need scarcely again express our great gratification over the favorable outcome."

The scandalous nature of this bribery of government officials could hardly be more clearly proved. Yet the letters *had* been stolen. And Hearst had kept them for three whole years before he chose to bring them to the public attention. People who doubted his motives charged that he was not a true reformer but an opportunist, a man who only exposed graft when it served his own purposes.

To make matters worse, during the course of the congressional investigation that followed the publication of the Archbold letters, there were indications that a number of them had been altered or forged.

Once again, doubt was cast upon Hearst, whose use of pyrotechnics to achieve his ends sometimes backfired on him. The question still to be asked was not about the value of his goals, but about the path he took in order to accomplish them.

Hearst's purposes were not achieved this time. Though there had never been any real hope that the Independent candidates—Thomas L. Hisgen for president and John Temple Graves for vice president—could actually win, the hope was that they would receive enough votes to demonstrate public awareness of the political corruption of members of both major parties. The Independent platform contained Hearst's recurrent demands for an eight-hour workday, control of monopolies, federal operation of the railroads, formation of a Department of Labor, a stronger Navy, and popular election of senators.

The Hearst press urged, "Vote for Hisgen, Graves, and Principle," adding, "The vote for principle is never thrown away." However, the Independence League candidates lost the presidential election to the Democratic candidate, William Howard Taft. They did not receive enough votes to even make a respectable showing.

Chapter 15

The Most
Hated Man

When the battleship U.S.S. *Maine* sank off Cuba in 1898 due to a mysterious explosion, Hearst, among others, was very vocal in his demands that the United States declare war against Spain.

Less than twenty years later, German torpedoes sank the giant British passenger ship, the *Lusitania*, on May 7, 1915, killing about 1,200 passengers, many of whom were American. In contrast to his earlier actions, Hearst argued *against* the entry of the United States into the war, although Hearst did condemn the sinking as "wholesale murder." In an editorial printed on June 6, 1915, Hearst wrote, "Whether the *Lusitania* was armed or not, it was properly a spoil of war, subject to attack and destruction under the accepted rules of civilized warfare. . . . The *Lusitania* incident is, of course, no cause for a declaration of war. No ten sane men in America want to see war with Germany. What sense is there in conduct and speech that might lead to war?"

It is said that Hearst simply hated England, although nobody is sure why he felt this way. His ancestors had come from England. One of Hearst's greatest detractors, Ferdinand Lundberg, wrote that Hearst "was in intimate association with German interests. . . . He was pro-German before the United States declared war." They cited Hearst's ownership of a German-language newspaper that he had bought, unknowingly, as part of the package when he took over the *New York Morning Journal.* Lundberg also spoke of Hearst's personal friendship with the German ambassador to the United States and with the kaiser. "But these friendships were merely surface reflections of deeper, material ties. Hearst's expansion, as it later developed, was financed by German-American bankers and brewers."

The anti-Hearst barrage set down by his detractors went on, insisting that the publisher was against the Allies because of his own sinister interests. It was also stated that once the war had started, Hearst gave "hypocritical lip-service to correct ideas, for private profit." These are inflammatory words, driven by a point of view that finds only evil in Hearst's heart. Others, trying to understand Hearst's insistence that America stay out of the war in Europe, said that he would have taken that stand if only to oppose the position of President Woodrow Wilson. It was said that if Wilson was fond of the English, Hearst would be compelled to dislike them.

There is no proof that Hearst's financial interests would have swayed him to side with Germany. Such actions would certainly have been out of character for Hearst, a man who spent years fighting for economic principles that were opposed to his own economic well-being. It has been suggested that Hearst had been introduced to a German who had influenced his thinking. It seems incredible that Hearst would have been susceptible to suggestions offered

※

Hearst was an "American Firster," unwilling to see the country embroiled in foreign affairs unless absolutely necessary.

by a mere acquaintance. His only close friend in Germany was Orrin Peck, a childhood companion, who had left Germany before the United States had entered the war. In fact, Peck had returned to San Francisco speaking ill of the Germans and their invasion.

Hearst was highly critical of the successful propaganda campaign that the Allies were waging across the United States. The British, who controlled the transatlantic cables, were able to spread vicious stories about Germany brutality, including one about how they cut off the hands of the enemy's children. This kind of propaganda caused such anger in the United States that anything that had a German name or attachment of any kind, including the small dogs called dachshunds, were abused. Hearst was very fond of these dogs. Indeed, he kept many of them around him over the years. He could not bear to see animals mistreated, and perhaps seeing dachshunds harmed, because of this hate-mongering, fueled his anti-British, pro-German sentiment. Mainly, however, Hearst was an "America First-er," unwilling to see the country become embroiled in foreign affairs unless absolutely necessary. And he did not believe anything was to be gained by entering into a war against Germany. Yet when he thought America or American interests were at risk, he changed from pacifist to antagonist. Indeed, he launched a propaganda effort of his own to persuade Americans to intervene in the civil strife taking place in Mexico.

While Willie Hearst was still in school, his father had become friends with Porfirio Diaz, president of Mexico, and had been able to buy a great deal of land there very cheaply. Hearst holdings included the million-acre Babicora ranch, in the Mexican state of Chihuahua. The ranch spread over four plateaus in the Sierra Madre mountain range, and 150 ranchers employed by Hearst tended thousands of head of cattle there.

Diaz had been driven out of Mexico by revolutionaries in 1911, and late in 1915 Pancho Villa's band raided the Hearst ranch, stole 60,000 head of cattle, and killed one worker while looting the property. Although the ranch belonged to his mother at the time, Hearst was incensed by the rebels' attack. He matched the anti-German propaganda with some of his own directed at Mexico. On December 22, 1913, the *New York American* ran a photograph of a group of children with their hands held high, apparently on an ocean beach. The story that accompanied this photo stated: "As proof of an almost unbelievable state of barbarity existing in Mexico . . . an English traveler, fellow of the Royal Geographical Society of London, sends the photograph shown here to the *American*. The children were driven into the water, forced to hold their hands above their heads, and shot in the back. The tide carried their bodies away. Note the terror in the face of the one child who partly faces the shore."

When the man who had taken the picture saw it in the newspaper, one could have noted the horror on *his* face, no doubt. The picture he had sent to the *American* had not even been taken in Mexico. It was taken at the shore in Honduras, the children were bathing, and the one with his face to the camera was simply curious about the man with the camera. The English traveler who took that snapshot was indignant, at the very least, to see his picture misrepresented.

While trying to keep the United States out of the war across the Atlantic, Hearst pushed to get the country into war south of the border. "MEXICANS PREPARE FOR WAR WITH U.S." shouted one headline in 1916. "Is it not time for the soldiers of the United States to do something PERMANENT? . . . Nothing worthwhile will be accomplished by occasional 'punitive' expeditions. . . . The way to IMPRESS the Mexicans is to REPRESS the Mexicans," his papers insisted. They went on to point out

that the attitude toward Mexico of Hearst publications . . . is the exact attitude which the Hearst publications maintained with reference to the Cuban situation, and there are no Hearst interests in Cuba . . . (it is necessary) that the United States government exercise the fundamental functions of all governments and protect its citizens; that it prevent the Mexicans from murdering any more of our citizens; and that it punish Mexico for the murders and outrages already committed upon our citizens and our soldiers."

Hearst went on to state his own perplexing, but not totally unbelievable logic, saying, "It would seem to me that anyone who was not an incurable idiot would see at a glance that I am incurring the greatest possible risk to any properties I or my family might have in Mexico by taking this stand, so objectionable to the powers in Mexico; and that nothing but a

Pancho Villa (1878–1923), second from the right, led rebellious troops and a guerrilla band during the Mexican Revolution.

89

strong sense of patriotic duty would impel a man to take a stand so offensive to a vicious and vindictive Mexican government. . . ."

Revenge against Mexico was not the only warlike foreign policy stand that Hearst took. He was also directing attention toward Japan, which was, he was persuaded, just waiting for an opportunity to take over the United States. This belief was fueled by information that a Japanese syndicate was about to buy land on the California coast. Hearst lobbied for resolutions reaffirming the Monroe Doctrine and opposing the ownership of land by a foreign country. The Japanese purchase was forestalled, as was another attempt made the next year over the border in Mexico.

As for his country's entry into World War I, here is what Hearst wrote about that many years later:

> I opposed our going into the war, and tried to unite the great journals of England and America to prevent the war.
>
> Once we were in, however, we had to win and bring the conflict to as speedy a conclusion as possible.
>
> Therefore I supported the draft and went down to Washington, D.C., and wrote in the *Washington Post*, and influenced my friends in Congress to vote for the draft. . . .
>
> I think I did the right things. At least I did the best I knew.
>
> We should have kept out of the war altogether, but that I could not accomplish, and I only got hated and berated for my pains.
>
> However, we do not mind that in the newspaper business. It is part of the game.

Chapter *16*

Undaunted

A story is told about a night
a Hearst advertising executive, A.J. Kobler, was
invited to Hearst's home at 86th Street and Riverside
Drive in New York City. Perhaps, from the window,
they could see Hearst's yacht moored in the Hudson
River. Certainly they could see the lights blinking on
the New Jersey Palisades, across the river.

Hearst asked his guest if he'd like a beer to
drink, and Kobler said that he would. Hearst rang
for a servant, but it was late and he got no answer.
The cabinets that held the refreshments were all
locked. At that point, Hearst went to the butler's
pantry and returned with a small axe. He proceeded
to break the locks on several cupboards, looking for
a beer, but he couldn't find any. The two men had
a glass of wine and sat chatting and drinking until
two o'clock in the morning.

Kobler was astounded at Hearst's behavior. That
afternoon, when he returned to Hearst's apartment

for a business meeting, he was even more surprised to discover that the cabinets were all in perfect repair. "No one could have guessed an axe had crashed them open twelve hours previously," he later said.

The story is symbolic of a man who would let very little stand in his way, and who continued on as if little had happened even if he did not achieve his goal. His disappointment with politics was serious; still he continued to wield whatever political power he could muster, and fight for the policies he believed in. His publishing ventures expanded greatly, yet he kept control over their operations to a degree that some of his employees found amazing if not frightening.

"Hearst himself makes it a point to keep a finger in every pie," wrote John K. Winkler in 1928, when Hearst was 65 years old. "Hearst's executives have a vast respect and very appreciable terror of their chief." Winkler continued, "Hearst derives Machiavellian delight in sitting on the side lines and relishing quarrels between the pawns on his chessboard. When he has had his fun, and is convinced the scrap has gone far enough, he takes a hand. Generally he 'suggests' a vacation to one or the other disputant."

Winkler relates one amusing incident in which one of the reporters failed to meet expectations and was told by the chief, as his newspaper employees called Hearst, to take a trip abroad. "Leaving Saturday for Egypt. Is that far enough?" the reporter queried his employer in a telegram.

The chief was a different Hearst from the one who threw parties for his workers on his San Francisco newspaper, and who kept his people energized and enthusiastic. But those were the days when the one thing in the world he wanted was to be a successful newspaper publisher. He had achieved that goal and had gone after others that he had not reached.

There is no doubt that William Randolph Hearst was a man who thrived on challenges and who wanted and achieved enormous power. He didn't

※

"Hearst derives Machiavellian delights in sitting on the side lines and relishing quarrels between the pawns on his chessboard."

want it for its own sake, though, or for self-aggrandizement. He wanted power in order to change the way things were done, in order to achieve greater equality for working people, and in order to overthrow the tyrannies of those whose wealth was used against the masses.

Hearst's social and political policies were advanced for his times, and liberal by most standards. He was even among the few who supported the issue of women's suffrage during the earliest years. In 1896 he had employed Susan B. Anthony, a leader of the women's movement, to write for his *San Francisco Examiner*. Articles in support of the militant British suffrage movement also appeared in the *Examiner*. "You cannot take a woman's son and send him to war to be shot, unless you give her the right to vote about that war," San Franciscans read in Hearst's paper. Women got the vote in California in 1911, nine years before the 19th amendment gave women the right to vote throughout the United States.

Hearst had been building up his newspaper chain and also had established the International News Service. In October 1915, *Harper's Weekly* magazine printed a story calling the INS reports from Europe fraudulent. The magazine had sent letters to Hearst's bylined reporters—those whose names were signed to the articles that appeared from abroad—and the letters were returned undelivered. According to *Harper's*, Hearst was using amateur writers and printing their stories under fictitious bylines.

The INS supplied news not only to Hearst papers, but also sold its services to other newspapers. Thus it was in direct competition with the largest American news syndicate, the Associated Press, a cooperative venture among all its members. In 1916, the AP took Hearst and INS to court for stealing its news stories and distributing or selling them as if that news had been gathered by INS. Hundreds of examples of such theft were offered in

In 1907, the Hearsts moved into the Clarendon Apartment House on Riverside Drive in New York City.

evidence and substantiated by showing, for instance, that a name misspelled in an AP story would be similarly misspelled when the story went out over INS wires.

Although the wrongdoing by INS was apparent, and the honor of the service was seriously tainted, Hearst was not forced to either pay damages or give up his membership in the Associated Press. Since Hearst owned so many newspapers that paid for and contributed to the AP, its directors didn't want to alienate him completely.

The INS was denied the privileges of the cables and mails during World War I because it had, as the British maintained, "garbled and distorted the news."

"I will apologize for nothing, retract nothing, alter nothing," Hearst wrote his INS editor.

"Therefore, I have nothing to retract or alter in the slightest degree. On the contrary, I wish to assure the English censorship and the English government that the Hearst publications will continue to pursue the same independent course that they have been pursuing with redoubled conviction of the truth, justice, and propriety of that course."

In addition to the news syndicate, Hearst owned seven newspapers and two magazines, and he continued to acquire more. In 1912 he bought two papers in Atlanta, Georgia, and in 1913 he took over another San Francisco paper: the *Morning Call*. It was editorially a conservative paper that had been founded in 1886. Hearst made it an evening paper and changed its editorial policies to match the rest of his liberal, progressive publications.

After doubling the circulation of *Cosmopolitan*, Hearst was persuaded by his financial advisers that the magazine should change its muckraking character. He agreed, and *Cosmopolitan*, between 1912 and 1918, changed its image to satisfy the popular taste, which had become tired and fed up with the shrill accusations of the muckrakers. The magazine concentrated more on romance, adventure, and mystery, incorporating sex into the articles and stories whenever possible.

In 1911 Hearst bought *Good Housekeeping*. His editor, Richard Waldo, in a brilliant stroke of genius, founded the Good Housekeeping Institute to test and approve mechanical devices. The Good Housekeeping Seal of Approval, guaranteeing the products of those advertisers who received it, was a boon to selling both products and the magazine itself. *Good Housekeeping* became the most successful woman's publication in the world, with a circulation of nearly two million.

Hearst bought an unsuccessful magazine called *The World To-day,* renamed it *Hearst's International Magazine,* and later merged it with *Cosmopolitan.* His success with *Cosmopolitan* and *Good Housekeeping* encouraged Hearst to buy *Harper's Bazar* in 1912. By 1900 at least ten Hearst magazines were aimed at women and their interests, including the *Ladies Home Journal,* as well as long-gone titles, such as *The Modern Priscilla. Harper's Bazar* (it did not add the extra "a" to become *Bazaar* until 1929) and *Vogue* had been published for 50 years by the very respectable publishing company of Harper & Brothers. *Vogue* was bought by Condé Nast in 1905, and when Hearst took over *Harper's Bazar* the battle lines were drawn. Hearst raided Nast's staff just as he had raided Pulitzer's. The rivalry became keen and has remained so ever since.

As he "collected" magazines and newspapers, Hearst also avidly collected art and antiques. The Hearsts had moved to the Clarendon, on the corner of Riverside Drive and 86th Street in New York City, in 1907. At the time of the move, walls were removed and the entire front of the building facing the river was made into one room. But there was not enough room for the things Hearst had been collecting, and he wanted to remove floors and reconstruct ceilings. To do so, he bought the building and created a vast, Gothic hall in which he housed his gleaming armor and hung his exquisite tapestry.

Hearst became interested in the young motion picture industry in 1913, and a few years later he met the woman who inspired him to throw himself into movie-making obsessively. His attachment to this young woman would also take him back to California, where he would build San Simeon—the most famous and extraordinary castle in America.

A Princess and a Castle

*T*he Ziegfeld Follies became an emblem of a glamorous, glittery era in American theater. The Follies was a theatrical review produced by Florenz Ziegfeld, a theatrical impresario who began booking acts for the Chicago World's Fair of 1893. He went on to stage musical comedies, and in 1907 he produced the first of the Follies—a variety show with everything from dancing girls to stand-up comics. It was modeled after the Folies Bergeres, a show that was the rage of Paris.

Many of the country's most famous performers appeared in the Ziegfeld productions, and it was the dream of young, stage-struck hopefuls to land a part in the Follies. One young woman whose dreams began to come true when she was discovered by Ziegfeld and given a place in a Follies chorus line was Marion Cecilia Davies.

She was born Marion Douras in Brooklyn, sometime around 1900. The exact date is not certain, but she was under 20 years old when William Randolph Hearst first met her. He was in his mid-fifties. Although he was a doting father and decent husband, he could not resist the attraction of the lovely young woman who was cheerful, fun-loving, funny, generous, and romantic. She could make him laugh and lift his spirits, which must certainly have been at their lowest ebb after the series of defeats he'd suffered, the elections he'd lost, and the war he could not stop. She won Hearst's heart, and she also fell in love with him. The rumor was that he attended the Follies every night for eight weeks, just to gaze at her. It was also said that he always bought two tickets, one seat for himself and the other for his hat.

Hearst had already started a movie production company when he met Marion Davies, but now he threw himself into making movies with special zeal. He was determined to make Miss Davies a star. He hired the best and most expensive tutors to teach her all the skills of acting. He involved himself in her

The Ziegfeld Follies were famous for their elaborate chorus numbers featuring a bevy of exotically costumed chorus girls.

A Princess and a Castle

career with incredible energy and determination, for he was a man who could not be stopped when he put his mind to something he wanted. He intended to see Marion Davies become the greatest and most acclaimed actress in the country and planned to be the wizard impresario who made it all happen. In truth, he had far greater aspirations for her than she did.

Hearst's Cosmopolitan Corporation produced two films in which Miss Davies starred during 1918, *Runaway Rosemary* and *Cecilia of the Pink Roses*. She was endlessly photographed by the Hearst newspapers, which also sang her praises. "Marion Davies Wins Triumph," read one headline. "There were few dry eyes at the Rivoli Theater yesterday when the vision of Marion Davies faded on the screen," said the review. "Only a marble heart could have withstood the charms of Marion Davies."

Although she was not ever a really good actress, that fact did not deter Hearst. He had a tendency to believe that things were, or at least could be, the way he wanted them to be. So he continued to promote a film career that had few sincere boosters.

The Hearst extravagance was unbounded and astounding when he became a movie producer. For a scene in *The Young Diana* (1921), which was supposed to take place in Switzerland, he had an ice skating rink built on the lot. But Marion Davies could not skate. She couldn't even stand up on ice. Champion figure skater Bobby McLean was brought in to skate on the ice, and when it was time for a close-up Marion Davies was held in place by two stage hands. When the movie was finished, Hearst didn't like the way it looked and the whole thing was done over, eliminating the ice and shooting the scenes in the snow.

When one of Hearst's movies opened in 1922, he had the theater in which it premiered completely and lavishly redecorated—even though the building didn't belong to him.

Marion Davies was Hearst's companion for more than thirty years.

A Princess and a Castle

In 1924 he produced *Janice Meredith,* a movie about the American Revolution, with a cast of about 7,500 people. More than 2,000 uniforms were made for the soldiers, and Marion Davies wore twenty gowns during the shooting. The whole company moved to upstate New York when they needed scenes in which snow was falling, and 46 houses were constructed there to represent the background. When they realized that real falling snow did not photograph well, a dozen men were hired to scatter 4,000 bags of confetti in front of whirling airplane propellers to give the impression of falling snow.

For the movie called *The Red Mill* (1927), an entire village was built to scale, modeled after photographs of a Dutch town. It was built around an artificial canal. For winter scenes, when the canal had to be frozen, a refrigeration system was constructed so that the water could be frozen, even beneath the Southern California sun.

Louella O. Parsons became the main movie reviewer for the Hearst press. She had been working for a non-Hearst newspaper when she wrote a glowing review of a Marion Davies performance. Hearst quickly hired her, more than doubling her salary.

Louella Parsons became a Hollywood dictator, insisting that films be screened for her alone when she prepared to review them. It was said that nobody in the movie business dared to have a large party without inviting Louella Parsons, and the life in Hollywood that Hearst and Marion Davies enjoyed was full of lavish entertaining.

Hollywood became the American movie capital after 1913. During the years of World War I, there were coal shortages and rationing of electricity in the East. Under such conditions, Southern California's agreeable climate and inexpensive land made Hollywood even more attractive to movie producers. Enormous studio lots appeared in and around Hollywood, which is part of the city of Los Angeles. One way to rank the importance of a movie star was by the relative opulence of his or her studio dressing room. Hearst joined forces with Metro-Goldwyn-Mayer movie studio, bringing Marion Davies with him. The studio built Miss Davies a fourteen-room "cottage" that was staffed with servants and furnished with antiques. Her "dressing room" became the headquarters for visiting dignitaries and the social center of the lot. As the movie industry grew during the 1920s, the name Hollywood became synonymous, not only with filmmaking, but also with glitter, glamour, and gossip, much of which was generated at the fabulous parties given for and by the beautiful people of the era.

At one Hollywood party, a special edition of Hearst's *Los Angeles Examiner* was printed to be handed out to all the guests. The entire front page was devoted to the partygoers. The standard subhead, "The Paper for People Who Think" was changed for the occasion to "The Paper for People Who Drink." By a peculiar quirk of fate, when the pressmen restored the real page to run off the next edition, they forgot to change the type of the subhead until after a few thousand copies of the paper had been printed and delivered.

William Randolph Hearst wanted very much to marry Marion Davies, but Millicent Hearst refused to grant him a divorce. Mrs. Hearst cited her Catholic faith, which would not permit her to divorce, and no doubt she was intent upon protecting the interests of her five sons. Despite the vast difference in their ages, and even though they could not be married, Hearst and Marion Davies remained together until the end of his life.

With all his movie activity and the continued expansion of his publishing empire, Hearst might have given up politics entirely. However, he remained involved in both New York and national political activities, attending conventions, and politicking in smoke-filled back rooms. But none of his important political dreams was to be fulfilled.

The main house, La Casa Grande, at San Simeon was designed by architect Julia Morgan in the Spanish Colonial style, and incorporated many of the treasures that Hearst had purchased in Europe.

However, he was to satisfy one of his long-term personal dreams—to build himself a castle at San Simeon in California. It was the family property he most cherished. Phoebe Hearst, his mother, became ill with the flu during a visit to New York City. She recovered and returned home to California, only to suffer a relapse. Her son and his wife went to the West Coast, and while they were there, Hearst spent time working with an architect on plans for the castle he wished to build. Mrs. Hearst died on April 13, 1919, and was buried beside her husband, the late senator. During her lifetime she had given more than $20 million to education and other causes in which she believed. She left an estate of $11 million, most of which her son inherited.

Within a few years, construction was begun on the three guest houses at San Simeon. The architect was a woman, Julia Morgan, well known for wearing large, old-fashioned hats and horn-rimmed glasses. Miss Morgan, a friend of Phoebe Hearst, was a graduate of the Ecole de Beaux Arts in Paris. She devoted her career to helping William Randolph Hearst make his dream come true.

The hill on which his castle was being built rose 2,000 feet above the Pacific Ocean. He named it *La Cuesta Encantada,* The Enchanted Hill. Each of the three guest houses was palatial, and these were completed before the castle, *La Casa Grande,* was begun. However, even the construction of the guest houses suffered setbacks when Hearst was dissatisfied. Once, when Hearst was driving up the private road that climbed the mountainside, he decided that a guest house under construction was not located correctly. He had it torn down and started again in a preferred location. A similar reluctance to accept anything that did not suit him perfectly led him to have the twin towers of the main castle torn down. He discovered that he liked them less in real life than when he had judged them on paper.

La Casa Grande was as extravagant, ornate, excessive, overbearing, and attention-getting as the man to whom it belonged. On the grounds of San Simeon was the largest private wild-animal preserve in the country, complete with elephants, tigers, water buffaloes, ostriches, yaks, and chimpanzees. Signs proclaimed that animals had the right-of-way, and one day a visitor had to wait an hour for a moose to finish sunning itself in the middle of the road.

The treasures Hearst had been collecting for over 50 years were stored in warehouses in New York and other storerooms. These treasures which included tapestries, statues, paneling, doors, staircases, stained glass, mantels, and columns were sent to California. In fact, entire rooms had been shipped home in anticipation of the great castle he would someday build.

In addition to the construction that went on over the years, with crews of as many as 150 men at a time, the landscape was being perfected by a head gardener who had 20 men working for him. Cypress trees 30 feet tall were brought in and planted. Hearst hated to see trees cut down, and he had several large oaks that stood in the way of construction moved to other sites, a time-consuming and very costly undertaking.

Famous visitors were always on the guest list at San Simeon. In 1929, while Winston Churchill was there, a maid rushed into the house saying that Mr. Churchill was fainting and wanted some turpentine. Hearst rushed out to the garden to discover Churchill, whose hobby was painting, seated at an easel puffing his ever-present cigar. It turned out that the maid had mistaken the gardener's message about Churchill needing turpentine.

The guest list at San Simeon was certainly one of the most celebrated in the entire country. On at least one occasion, the company present was surprised with an invitation to travel, as Hearst's guest, on some European or South American adventure. "On these trips Mr. Hearst is just like a boy out of school," wrote one of the guests who accompanied him on an excursion to Germany. "He makes me feel at least old enough to be his mother. He jokes with the boatmen and the itinerant musicians, does a little yodeling on his own account, and buys wooden animals and carved inkstands, and gaily colored scarves and sweaters, and sweets and wines and cheeses—whatever there is to buy, in fact, and all the time tells us in the most interesting way the history of all the places we visit."

Bad Politics and Bad Paperwork

*D*espite the attractions of California, Hearst continued to be a force in New York state politics, and after the election of 1918, he used his influence against Governor Alfred E. Smith. The publisher's grudge against the governor went back to 1907, when young Smith had allied himself with "Big Tom" Foley, a Tammany district head whom Hearst opposed. Then, in 1918, when Hearst sought the governorship, it was Smith who beat him for the post.

Not that Hearst's political animosities were personal grudges—the Smith children had been invited to play with the Hearst children on certain occasions, and Hearst was well-known as a fence-mender when the mood struck him. Hearst had, indeed, supported the governor when Smith promised to support one of Hearst's favored causes: government ownership of transportation and public utilities.

However, Smith had been dragging his feet on that score, according to Hearst. And just possibly Hearst was also jealous of Smith's growing popularity.

In that atmosphere of mistrust, the Hearst press began charging Governor Smith with responsibility for a serious shortage of milk that continued after a strike by milk producers had been settled. They called it a "milk scandal" and said that children were starving because of Smith's alliance with the "Milk Trust." There were dreadful cartoons showing starving children, and the blame was directed at Smith.

Smith angrily retorted, calling Hearst "a mean man, a particularly low type of man," and challenged Hearst to a public debate. Smith supporters rented Carnegie Hall for the night of October 29, 1919. Hearst was sent an official invitation to stand up on the platform and, as Smith said, "ask me any question he likes about my public or about my private life, if he will let me do the same."

The challenge was turned down, perhaps, in part, because Hearst was unwilling to have his private life, in which Marion Davies played a leading part, discussed in public. He answered Smith: ". . . I have no intention of meeting Governor Smith privately, politically, or socially.

"I do not have to meet him as I am not running for office; and I certainly do not want to meet him for the pleasure of association, as I find no satisfaction in the company of crooked politicians.

"Neither have I time or inclination to debate with every plunderer or faithless public servant whom my papers have exposed. . . .

"And, in conclusion, let me say that if you . . . are going to hire Carnegie Hall every time my papers expose rascally politicians, you would better take a long-term lease on the property."

Smith was a "self-made" man who had been born into a poor family with the gift of making people laugh. He also had a link of interest and affection for common people. He was not polished, nor did he speak with refinement or good grammar, but he was burning to take Hearst on for those unfair accusations. Smith took the stage at Carnegie Hall and announced:

"I am going to ask for your absolute silence and attention. I feel that I am here tonight upon a mission as important not only to myself, but to this city, to this state, and to this country, as I could possibly perform. . . . I know the man to whom I issued the challenge, and I know that he has not got a drop of good, clean, pure red blood in his whole body. . . ."

Smith berated Hearst for pretending to know what was happening in New York when he spent his winters in Florida and his summers in California. He went on to ask, "What can it be about me that I should be assailed in this reckless manner by this man? I have more reason probably than any man I will meet tonight to have a strong love . . . for this country, for this state, and for this city. Look at what I have received at its hands: I left school and went to work before I was fifteen years of age. I worked hard, night and day; I worked honestly and conscientiously at every job that I was ever put at, until I went to the governor's chair in Albany. Then, what can it be? It has to be jealousy, it has got to be envy, it has got to be something that nobody understands."

In conclusion, Smith urged his audience to organize and stop "the danger that comes from (Hearst's) papers, to the end that . . . we may get rid of this pestilence that walks in the darkness."

All of the latent resentment against Hearst began to coalesce around Alfred E. Smith, who was a daunting foe. He was winning the battle of words and gaining support for his stand. And in later years, even when Hearst made overtures of friendship, Smith held on to his angry defiance of the publisher. He refused again and again to be won over, either by advances from Hearst, or from Tammany, which was frequently ready to bow to Hearst's power in order to win favorable words in his newspapers.

Alfred E. Smith (1873–1944) won the 1918 election for governor of New York over Hearst and became one of his most feared opponents.

Bad Politics and Bad Paperwork

In 1922, during the Democratic state convention in Syracuse, New York, Hearst supporters attempted to work out an agreement with Smith through the Tammany people. Hearst was ready to support Smith for governor if Smith would give Hearst a Senate nomination.

"I'm damned if I will," was Smith's reply. His anger was still deep and he wouldn't run on the same ticket as the man he hated, and no one could persuade him otherwise. "Say, do you think I haven't any self-respect?" he asked when some party regulars tried to talk him into a deal. "You can tell Murphy I won't run with Hearst on the ticket and that goes!"

William Randolph Hearst had most certainly lost his political grip on the national scene. And even stranger things were going on relative to his affairs abroad. From November 14 to December 10, 1927, the Hearst newspapers published a series of articles that were based on secret documents. These documents were part of a Mexican plot to bribe four United States senators. Among the intrigues supposedly revealed by the papers were Russian-Japanese-Mexican plots against the United States.

Hearst was most anxious that his vast properties in Mexico be protected. Earlier, he had tried to instigate a U.S. invasion of Mexico and failed. Those with reason to mistrust Hearst's intentions cited his self-interest in discrediting Mexico's leaders. Shortly before the existence of these "documents" was revealed, the Mexican government had passed land laws levying higher taxes on foreign landowners who were also going to be forced to give up their mining rights.

As expected, the Senate began an investigation to find out about the senators who were supposed to have taken bribes. In the course of these hearings, Hearst had to take the witness stand.

"Did you investigate whether money had actually been paid to the United States senators?" he was asked.

"No, sir, we didn't."

"Did you go to the senators mentioned and ask them?" the questioning went on.

"No," said Hearst. "We could not do so without revealing the contents."

"Have you any evidence that any senator received any such money as mentioned here?"

"No. In fact I do not believe they did receive any money," Hearst answered.

And, "Have you ever heard of any evidence to sustain such a charge?"

"No," Hearst confessed, "I do not believe the charge."

Yet it had appeared in his own newspapers. These were documents he had bought and published, without regard to their authenticity. That was one of the worst possible journalistic sins. Moreover, it developed, in time, that the documents were all forgeries, that Hearst had been duped, perhaps all too willingly.

The scandalous Mexican documents were fake, but some other papers Hearst got his hands on were not. This document was a secret agreement between England and France, in which each country promised to support the other. It was signed without the knowledge of the American government and when Hearst got hold of it he published it, to the horror of both those countries.

Two years later, in September 1930, when he was in Paris, Hearst found himself an unwelcome visitor, and was asked to leave the country. According to the French government's explanation of the expulsion, "William Randolph Hearst, proprietor of numerous newspapers in America, was expelled yesterday from French territory. This measure had as its origin the role played last year by Mr. Hearst in obtaining and publishing a secret document relating to the Anglo-French naval negotiations."

Edmond D. Coblentz, a friend of Hearst who was present, described what happened. "A French official handed Mr. Hearst his *congé* (abrupt dis-

❋
"William Randolph Hearst, proprietor of numerous newspapers in America, was expelled yesterday from French territory."

109

missal) in the corridor of the hotel. Immediately after receiving it, Mr. Hearst asked me to ride with him in his automobile. There was silence for a moment while he sat strumming his fingers on his knees, a characteristic gesture when he was deep in thought. Then he said to me quietly:

'The French government has ordered me to leave France.'

'What a foolish thing for them to do,' I commented.

'It was silly,' he replied. 'I am not remaining here. I am leaving this afternoon.'

"I accompanied him to the Gare du Nord, where, seemingly unperturbed, he walked up and down the platform munching peaches. I waited, and when the train pulled out, I glimpsed him seated in his compartment writing in longhand."

This is part of Hearst's reply, which he was probably composing as the train pulled out of the Gare du Nord:

". . . They said I was an enemy of France and a danger in their midst. They made me feel quite important. . . .

"They said I could stay in France a little while longer if I desired, that they could take a chance on nothing disastrous happening to the republic.

"But I told them that I did not want to take the responsibility of endangering the great French nation; that America had saved it once during the war, and I would save it again by leaving."

Hearst went on in that vein, taking the high moral ground as was his habit saying, "If being a competent journalist and loyal American makes a man *persona non grata* in France, I think I can endure the situation without loss of sleep."

Chapter 19

World War and
a Legacy

*H*earst's financial empire was made up of more than newspapers and magazines. It also included paper companies, a chain of radio stations, film and theater investments, real estate, cattle ranch and fruit properties, canning and packing plants, and mining enterprises, both in the United States and abroad.

When the great stock market crash of 1929 came and millions of people were unemployed, Hearst urged President Herbert Hoover to stimulate prosperity by making a $5 billion loan to those who were out of work. He also advocated the six-hour workday. "The first duty of this government is to give the workers work. They will give trade to the shops and orders to industries. They will pay rents, buy shoes and clothing, and put money into circulation." Hearst wanted the government to spend money on public works, and he also believed that farmers should receive federal financing in the form of low-cost loans. This money would allow them to get back on their feet. The Hoover Administration followed none of his advice.

Hearst's political influence reached its peak in the early part of the century and declined to its lowest point when Alfred E. Smith refused to drop his grudge against the publisher. Many years later, when Hearst threw his weight behind the presidential nomination of Franklin D. Roosevelt, at Smith's expense, it may have been that Hearst finally felt vindicated against Smith.

Politically, Hearst changed as he grew older, becoming more conservative. He was less favorably inclined toward labor unions, especially when they wanted a role to play in his own publishing ventures. He grew to have little enthusiasm for income taxes, which he now declared to be a "racket." He suggested a sales tax instead. He now believed it was time to keep cheap foreign goods out of the American market, a different stand from his earlier one, which was against protective tariffs.

Hearst was in control of the votes that swung the Democratic presidential nomination in 1932, and with a telephone call was able to assure victory for Franklin Delano Roosevelt. W.R. Hearst had actually named a president for the first time. Yet he found himself in opposition to the measures Roosevelt was taking to bring the country out of the Great Depression of the 1930s.

In 1928, John K. Winkler's biography, *W.R. Hearst: An American Phenomenon*, was published. Winkler had been a reporter on Hearst's *New York American*. The book, which was a friendly examination of the publisher's life, attracted great national attention. A friend recommended to Hearst that he read it, but he declined saying, "If it doesn't tell the truth it will make me mad, and if it tells the truth it will make me sad."

On April 29, 1933, William Randolph Hearst celebrated his seventieth birthday, telegrams bearing congratulations arrived from all over the world. Friends gathered at San Simeon to wish him well. "I am not thinking about my seventieth birthday. It is much like any other day," Hearst said. "My mind is on my hundredth birthday. I am glad you came today, and I thank you. I invite you all to dine here with me in 1963."

Although he remained on courteous terms with his wife, Millicent, and saw his sons and their families regularly, he lived out the rest of his life with Marion Davies, to whom he remained devoted. He did make her a famous screen star, although she never was a great one. And he made her rich. Indeed, when Hearst, at the age of seventy-four, suffered serious financial reversals, Davies dug into her bank account and produced $1 million to help him out of trouble.

Hearst had begun his career in newspapers with a substantial fortune inherited from his father. During the course of his career, he collected newspapers and then magazines as obsessively as he collected antiques. The financial history of his newspaper empire is as tangled and complex and as difficult to assess as was any effort to catalogue his vast holdings of antiques, in which junk was mixed in with valuable treasures. The assumption was that Hearst was always making another fortune with his papers, but that is questionable. By 1924, five years before the Wall Street Crash and the Great Depression of the 1930s, Hearst's papers were costing more than they were earning. But nobody seemed to know what was going on at the time. In October 1935, *Fortune* magazine published a story praising the way the Hearst organization had come through the crash and the Depression and recommending the company's stock. Less than two years later, the company was on the brink of bankruptcy, showing just how wrong the financial magazine had been.

A network of corporations had been formed to handle the financial affairs of Hearst's various properties. Things were so bad by 1937 that Hearst relinquished control of his publishing enterprises, which were $126 million in debt. Those in charge did what Hearst himself never would. They sold several of his newspapers, some real estate, and even his treasures. The entire fifth floor of Gimbel's department store in New York City was cleared of regular merchandise and filled with the objects Hearst had collected over the years, from doorknobs to portraits of royalty. The sale was a spectacle for voyeurs and bargain hunters alike. It was estimated that for about fifty years, William Randolph Hearst had spent about one million dollars each year on his art collection. He also had bought six castles.

Saved from complete disaster by stern management, the Hearst publishing ventures were finally brought back from the edge of disaster by the prosperity that came with the advent of World War II.

In 1923, when his empire was intact, Hearst owned twenty-two daily newspapers and fifteen Sunday papers. When he died there were sixteen dailies and two Sundays left.

More books about Hearst were published. Some depicted him as an ogre who was moved to action only by self-interest. Others revered him as a man who had taken up the welfare of the great majority of the people with a missionary zeal. Some writers portrayed him as a publishing genius who succeeded by giving the public what it wanted. Others challenged that idea, saying that his wealth came not from his publishing genius, but from giving the public what it wanted—on the assumption that it wanted the worst.

In 1941 the Orson Welles movie, *Citizen Kane*, came out and created an uproar. When he heard that *Citizen Kane* might hurt his friend, Louis B. Mayer, the head of Metro-Goldwyn-Mayer, offered $800,000 to keep the film from being shown. M.G.M. was the studio which distributed Hearst's films, and where Marion Davies had made several films.

Nelson Rockefeller, son of the oilman John D. and owner of Rockefeller Center and the Radio City Music Hall, banned *Citizen Kane*. When asked about it, Rockefeller said that Louella Parsons had called him and told him to ban the movie. The Hearst press never reviewed it. Yet, in time, *Citizen Kane* overcame resistance and even won the citation for Best Picture of the Year. It has been praised as a cinematic masterpiece, and it is considered to be a popular biography of the man. Certainly it lodges in the mind of anyone who sees it and seems to take on the weight of reality. Yet it is just one interpretation, one artist's psychological portrait of W.R. Hearst.

Hearst and his activities were the subject of other fictional and nonfictional endeavors. *The Front Page*, which was a play and later a movie, was based in part upon events that took place in Hearst's *Chicago Herald* and *Examiner*. The English writer Aldous Huxley published *After Many a Summer Dies the Swan*, a novel about an American millionaire modeled after Hearst, who had a phobia about growing old. This idiosyncrasy is caricatured in Huxley's story, in which the main character, an aging millionaire, has scientists working to prolong his life. Ilka Chase made Hearst into a sinister individual in her book *Past Imperfect*. She wrote about the affair of a millionaire and a young beauty. Her book especially angered Hearst because the author and her mother had both been guests at San Simeon.

During the summer of 1934, Hearst made a trip to Germany that was to cast a long shadow on his political persona. At the end of his trip, in September, Hearst met with Adolf Hitler, whom he praised as a bulwark against Communism. He even brought home a contract to publish articles by one of Hitler's closest associates, Hermann Goering. Disguised as news, these articles were really Nazi propaganda.

His supporters said that Hearst was just politically naïve and allowed his hatred of Communism to stand in the way of him recognizing just how evil

William Randolph Hearst and Marion Davies traveled to Germany in 1934.

Hitler's fascist philosophy was. Hearst's detractors said that he was plainly revealing his own fascist leanings. There is really little evidence that Hearst supported Hitler's anti-Semitism, however. The most ardent position Hearst took, besides anti-Communism, was the same one he had taken before World War I: a stand against the United States entering the war. "Be neutral. Be American. Keep the United States out of the war," Hearst instructed his editors.

Not long after that, President Franklin Roosevelt remarked at a news conference that most of the opposition to his policies came from the Soviet and

Nazi press, the Republican National Committee, and the Hearst newspapers. "The Hearst papers are never quite sure that they can support or oppose the president's policies, because those policies change so much on their way from expression to execution," Hearst retorted in print. "But we are quite sure that we oppose Russian Communism, German Nazism, and English and French imperialism. We support American liberty and democracy, American freedom of the press and freedom of speech, including freedom of the president to take a few fireside shots occasionally."

This was vintage Hearst. It made Roosevelt chuckle.

When Japan attacked Pearl Harbor on December 7, 1941, the United States found itself at war with Japan and with Germany and its allies. Early in the war, Hearst closed San Simeon and moved to another of his manor houses in northern California called Wyntoon. This move was made to save money and because it was feared that the Japanese, long a target of Hearst propaganda, might find San Simeon an accessible military target from the bay that it overlooked. For two years, he and Marion Davies lived at Wyntoon, a remote and solitary place which she didn't like at all. Hearst was at Wyntoon for his seventy-ninth birthday party, and his executives made a trek to the backwoods to honor their "chief."

Hearst's eightieth birthday, in 1943, was celebrated at the beach house in Santa Monica, California, that Hearst had built for Marion Davies. As if in defiance of his mortality, Hearst wore a colorful paisley vest, silk tie, and flashy jacket. When the war ended in 1945, Miss Davies sold the Santa Monica house and the couple moved back to San Simeon. In 1947 Hearst suffered a painful and serious heart seizure, and his health began its final decline. He was forced to leave his beloved San Simeon and move closer to the city and his physicians. He wept as he left San Simeon for the last time.

William Randolph Hearst spent the final four years of his life in a relatively modest house in Beverly Hills. He died at the age of eighty-eight on the morning of August 14, 1951. Marion Davies had been tending to him and had stayed at his bedside most of the night before. Finally, she went to sleep and a nurse discovered that Hearst had stopped breathing. Instead of waking Miss Davies, the doctor who was called in contacted the family. She was still asleep when the undertaker arrived to take the body away. Hearst's relatives took over the funeral arrangements and ignored Miss Davies entirely, not acknowledging the more than thirty years she had spent with Hearst. He was buried in the marble Hearst mausoleum at Cypress Lawn Cemetery in Colma, just south of Los Angeles.

Hearst's will filled 125 pages, and it carefully kept corporate control away from his five sons, all in their thirties and forties. The action was curiously similar to the way his own father deprived him of an immediate, direct inheritance. Although he left Marion Davies no bequest in his will, he had provided for her financial security in a trust fund drawn earlier. What she did end up with, to the astonishment of his family, were enough shares in the Hearst corporation to give her voting supremacy. However, after a good deal of legal maneuvering, that was relinquished and a compromise arranged.

Today, the Hearst publishing empire is stronger than ever. It is the country's biggest publisher of monthly magazines, with a net worth estimated at about $3.5 billion. William Randolph Hearst's grandson, Will Hearst III, now leads the corporation's flagship paper, the *San Francisco Examiner*. In a television commercial promoting the newspaper, there is a scene in which the ghost of the chief asks his grandson, "Are you sure you know what you're doing, Will?

"I don't know," replies Will III. "Did you?"

Chapter 20

The Imprint of an Impresario

"W.R. was a great man. Those who thought otherwise just didn't know him." These words were spoken by a woman who could well have hated William Randolph Hearst, since he left her when he fell in love with another woman. But they were spoken by his wife, Millicent Hearst, eight years after her husband had died.

He inspired fierce hatred and fierce loyalty. Most of the books written about him delved into his business and personal affairs, in order to judge him either an inspired leader or a dreadful despot. Those who despised him and his methods say that everything he did was for his own financial benefit and self-aggrandizement. On the other side of the argument are interpreters who say his motives were honorable and his methods, if sometimes excessive, were nevertheless often effective.

W.A. Swanberg's book, *Citizen Hearst*, published in 1961, is the most careful, thorough, unbiased exploration of the life of this man. Swanberg weighed all sides and all opinions carefully, examined all the evidence, and still came away saying, "Even today, a decade after his death and almost a century after his birth, the lock of his character is still unpickable. One gets only a partial view through the keyhole."

Even Swanberg's book became controversial. A. J. Liebling, the most renowned critic of the press, reviewed Swanberg's book with sharp criticism. He even found the book dangerous, saying that the biographer seems to accept the notion that Hearst was admirable in any way:

"What I think is perilous about any myth concerning Hearst is that it may creep into common acceptance as fact. The most dangerous myth about him is that he was a genius, or even a good newspaperman, because it might lead to the erroneous conclusion that he ran newspapers the right way, or that the way he ran them is the way to make money. The latter delusion might be the most dangerous of all."

Dangerous, perhaps, but it is still true that the most vulgar and disgusting of publications do make money.

What about "Rosebud," the last word uttered by the fictional W.R. Hearst in the movie, *Citizen Kane?* Rosebud was a sled that represented the boy's lost childhood, his sad separation from his parents, and his futile search for love. The theme of the movie is that Kane/Hearst was the way he was in an effort to be loved, but that the reason he could never find love was that he never had any to give. That seems a simplistic notion. Besides, the relationship of Hearst and Marion Davies seemed as close to love as most people are likely to get. Whatever it was that drew them to one another held them together for more than 30 years.

Many of the social and political reforms for which Hearst fought in his early days have been instituted, but many of the same battles are still being fought. Taxes, import tariffs, the power of the government versus the power of private enterprise, graft, isolationism versus involvement in the affairs of foreign countries, even the Panama Canal, are issues that were hotly argued during Hearst's day and continue to be argued today.

As for his newspapers, they did not present the news with any pretense at serious objectivity. They used news as a means of entertainment and of inciting readers to action. They were used by their publisher to promote political candidates, especially himself, and to push for the ideas and reforms in which he believed. One man who worked for Hearst said, "A Hearst newspaper is like a screaming woman running down the street with her throat cut." This vivid image describes the raw sensationalism of a Hearst paper.

Hearst's own views, expressed in instructions to his editors, are in confusing contrast to that description. "Make a paper for the nicest kind of people— for the great middle class," he wrote. ". . . Omit things that will offend nice people. Avoid coarseness and slang and a low tone. The most sensational news can be told if it is written properly . . .

"Do not exaggerate.

"Make the paper helpful and kindly. Don't scold and forever complain and attack in your news columns. Leave that to the editorial page.

"Be fair and impartial."

Despite what others thought, William Randolph Hearst probably believed that he was following those admirable tenets of journalism.

Although he was a capitalist of incredible talent and power, he was not a pioneer. He did not invent sensationalism, or what has come to be known as yellow journalism. Rather, he saw it in practice, decided that it was effective, and practiced it more successfully than anyone else. He was not an inventor; he was an impresario.

What was his effect on the journalistic world? "No man in history has had a greater impact on American journalism or contributed more to its sturdiness or devoted himself more unceasingly to making it the nerve center of American patriotism," wrote the president of a competing journalistic enterprise upon Hearst's death. And that same newspaper editorialized, "William Randolph Hearst was one of the most controversial figures of our times, and he left a vast imprint on journalism and on American life."

What kind of imprint?

Press critic A.J. Liebling, who despised what Hearst stood for in journalism, conceded that Hearst changed the nature of American journalism radically. This he did, Liebling said, with money. He took the fortune his father had earned and used it like a "heavy club" to get what he wanted and to build his publishing empire.

"It was a concept as simple as a very big bankroll in a very small crap game," Liebling wrote shortly after Hearst died. "There were one or two fortunes of a few million dollars apiece in the newspaper field when Hearst, at the age of twenty-three, decided to go into it, but they had been made in newspapers, by men who started with little. . . .

"He bought talent the way he bought art—indiscriminately. . . .

"Great or not," Liebling concluded, "Hearst was the man who changed the rules of American journalism. He made it so expensive to compete that no mere working newspaperman has been able to found an important paper in this century."

Those words have the ring of truth. The press today is owned largely by huge syndicates. Very few individually owned or family owned newspapers survive. Indeed, the cost of competing in the newspaper world has reduced the number of papers to the point where very few cities in the country have more than one, or at the most two, competing newspapers. When a newspaper has no competition, most of the incentive to do a good job is lost. A one-newspaper town becomes a town where much of the important news may go unreported.

Certainly Hearst had virtues—and a lot of faults. His worst fault was that he lied when truth stood in the way of what he wanted. His other moral principles left a great deal to be desired, as well. His greatest virtues were that, although he could have lived out his days as a lazy, self-indulgent millionaire, he chose to work, and he worked as hard as if he were struggling to make a living. Other good points had to do with the long battles he waged in support of the underprivileged, his sense of humor, his enjoyment of life, his loyalty, and his generosity to those he admired and considered friends.

Only this is certain: William Randolph Hearst, whether he was good or evil, great or petty, did, most assuredly, make his mark in history.

Bibliography

Brady, Kathleen. *Ida Tarbell, Portrait of a Muckraker.* New York: Seaview/Putnam, 1984.

Carlson, Oliver, and Ernest Sutherland Bates. *Hearst, Lord of San Simeon.* New York: The Viking Press, 1936.

Coblentz, Edmond D. (editor). *William Randolph Hearst: A Portrait in His Own Words.* New York: Simon & Schuster, 1952.

Lundberg, Ferdinand. *Imperial Hearst, A Social Biography.* New York: Equinox Cooperative Press, 1936.

Older, Mrs. Fremont. *William Randolph Hearst, American.* New York: Appleton-Century Company, 1936.

Steffens, Lincoln. *Autobiography.* New York: Harcourt, Brace and Company, 1931.

Swanberg, W.A. *Citizen Hearst.* New York: Charles Scribner's Sons, 1961.

Tebbel, John. *The Life and Good Times of William Randolph Hearst.* New York: E.P. Dutton & Co., 1952.

Winkler, John K. *W.R. Hearst: An American Phenomenon.* New York: Simon & Schuster, 1928.

Index

Acknowledgments and Credits

Frontispiece and pages 2, 12, 13, 17, 24, 31, 35, 55, 63, 79, 82, 89, 99, Brown Brothers.

Pages 6, 50, 116, Bettman Archive.

Page 21, New York Public Library Picture Collection.

Pages 34, 37, 40, 48, 74, 102, 107, AP/Wideworld.

Pages 41, 66, 78, 98, Culver Pictures.

Page 94, The New-York Historical Society, New York City.